Unlikely Gifts

Other Christmas Books by J. Ellsworth Kalas

The Christmas People
Christmas Reflections
The Scriptures Sing of Christmas
The Best Songs Come at Night
Christmas from the Back Side

Other Books by David Kalas

When Did God Become a Christian?
The Gospel According to Leviticus, forthcoming

DEVOTIONS FOR

Unlikely Gifts

THE HOLIDAY SEASON

J. Ellsworth Kalas

Compiled by David Kalas and Taddy Kalas

ABINGDON PRESS
NASHVILLE

UNLIKELY GIFTS
DEVOTIONS FOR THE HOLIDAY SEASON

Library of Congress Cataloging-in-Publication Data has been requested.

ISBN 978-1-5018-6972-3

18 19 20 21 22 23 24 25 26 27—10 9 8 7 6 5 4 3 2 1

MANUFACTURED IN THE UNITED STATES OF AMERICA

Contents

Contents

Introduction

*O*ur father ministered in so many ways. He taught, he pastored, he sang, he led, he counseled, he wrote. But above all, he preached. He felt his call to preach when he was still just a boy, and he began his preaching while still in his adolescent years. It would be a fair estimate to say that there were nearly eighty years between his first sermon and his last.

Many folks who were never part of Ellsworth Kalas's congregations and who never heard him preach were introduced to him through his many books. He came to publishing comparatively late in life. Yet even his writing was, for him, an extension of his preaching. "When you've written a book," he liked to say, "you can be preaching even while you sleep."

This book is born out of the preaching of Ellsworth Kalas. For thirty-eight years he pastored local churches in Wisconsin and Ohio, preaching to a church family every Sunday morning. He preached through every season of the year, year after year. So he preached through nearly forty Christmas seasons for the churches that he served.

We have culled the sermon manuscripts that we inherited from those years of celebrating Christmas with his congregations. And in this book, we are sharing with you selections from the good tidings of great joy that Ellsworth Kalas preached as a pastor. We trust that these selections will be a blessing to your own celebration of the season this year. And as they bless you, he will be preaching even while he sleeps.

Finally, there is one more word that ought to be said.

The son or daughter of a preacher—the so-called preacher's kid—is short one formative person in his or her life. That is to say, while another child raised in the church has both a pastor at church and a parent at home, for the preacher's kid those two important roles are both played by one individual. That's an enormous weight of responsibility for one person. And, candidly, any hypocrisy observed in the close quarters of family living can serve to undermine the public proclamation from the pulpit.

As his children, we want you to know that life and message were in perfect harmony in Ellsworth Kalas. There was no jarring disconnect. There was no troubling distance between what we heard and what we saw. His love, his patience, his wisdom, his peace, and his joy made his parenting just as much a blessing as his preaching.

December 1

The Unlikely Gift
of a Promise

_I_f I were to play a word association game, asking for your first reaction to a series of words, there's a good chance you would respond to "Christmas" with either "presents" or some variation on the word "giving." And that's right enough. After all, Christmas began with a gift. But it began with an unlikely gift: the gift of a promise.

But who wants a promise? About the only people who like promises are those who give them. Politicians find them useful, and so do debtors. People who are enjoying a relationship but aren't ready to be tied down like promises. Sports fans know all about promises. But it's more fun to give promises than to receive them, isn't it? It wouldn't be too satisfying to unwrap a great collection of beautiful presents only to find that each one contained a neat little promissory note.

But that's the way Christmas began—with a promise. Consider the familiar prophecy from Isaiah: "The people that walked in darkness have seen a great light . . . For unto us a child is born, unto us a son is given: and the government shall be upon his shoulder: and his name shall be called Wonderful, Counsellor, The mighty God, The everlasting Father, The Prince of Peace" (Isaiah 9:2a, 6 KJV).

That wasn't the only Christmas promise. Some Bible scholars say that there are scores, perhaps a hundred or more, in the Old Testament scripture. Classical Bible students say that the first promise came with the first evidence of human need. After that first act of human disobedience in Eden, the world caved in: there would be frustration in work, pain in childbirth, and the human race would be under a death sentence. But with all this disaster, a promise: the Seed of the woman would bruise the serpent's head. It was a strange, almost contradictory phrase. After all, the seed is normally the male share of the reproductive process. But classical scholars saw in this phrase a direct reference to the virgin birth of the Messiah. As far as his earthly line was concerned, the Promised One would be the product of a woman alone.

So the Christmas promise is an old promise, as old as the human race. As soon as our race got itself into a predicament where it needed the gift of Christmas, it received the gift of—a promise. So the people of Israel waited, generation after generation, holding to a promise.

A wise man in Israel said that "hope deferred makes the heart sick" (Proverbs 13:12a NKJV). I wonder how often the Israelites lost hope. A promise can become a tedious thing, a point of contempt and resentment, if nothing comes of it. New prophets would add an insight here or a phrase there, around which the faithful would rally with new hope. But always and always, it was only a promise.

And then, there was Christmas. The promise was fulfilled. Simeon said so. "I am ready to die now," he said, "because my eyes have seen the salvation of God." Others saw it, too. Wise men, who hailed him as a unique king, saw it. And an old woman named Anna, who had been praying all of her life for the redemption of God; when she saw the baby Jesus, she gave thanks to God and passed the good news to many like her in Jerusalem who had been waiting for the promise to be fulfilled.

Since then, millions of people, in every corner of the earth, have found the promise fulfilled in him—an endless line of splendor, made up of wonderfully different parts. And when all these people met Jesus Christ, they realized that he was the answer to the promise.

But note this: God's Christmas promise is fulfilled only for those who accept it. For all of these centuries, since the first Christmas, there have been people who have lived and died without the benefit of the promise. Millions of people in our country will celebrate this season, yet they go through life as if the promise had never happened.

We shouldn't be surprised. A promise is only as good as the one who makes it and as the willingness of another to accept it. I met a man on a park bench once; his life was pretty much a shambles. He explained that his father had promised him a college education and a place in the family business, but the young man had turned his back on it. A missionary doctor went to work in an area of India where cataracts were almost epidemic. He promised to restore sight to those who would come to him, and hundreds of persons did so. But hundreds of others continued in their failing vision and blindness because they wouldn't test the doctor's promise. No matter how sound a promise is, it will do no good unless a person receives it.

That's part of the poignancy of the Christmas season. For many, the gift of God lies under the Christmas tree, still wrapped. How sad! Even the promise of God is no good unless we give it a chance.

The very nature of a promise is that you have to gamble your faith on it. Some who look at the Christmas package have been disappointed so often in the past that they don't want to take the gamble. Others are too proud to admit that they need a present, even a Divine present, and they leave the promise untouched. Still others are so preoccupied with insignificant, competing presents that they never get around to the key gift, and the Eternal Promise lies neglected. You must use your faith to take the promise, to dare to unwrap it, to expose yourself to possible disappointment and ridicule. You have to gamble on the promise.

I appeal to you early in this season to gamble on Christmas.

December 2

The Long View

When I was a boy, the wait for Christmas seemed endless. The newspapers in our city carried a little front-page box through the season that advised the number of shopping days until Christmas. The figure was meant to encourage people to shop while there was still time, but for my childish mind it simply recorded the slow, tedious countdown until the big day. I still remember the disappointment I felt when I discovered that the figure was not accurate for my purposes. In those days stores were not open on Sundays, so when the papers reported the number of shopping days until Christmas, they were not telling us how long until Christmas itself. It might be fourteen shopping days but still be sixteen or seventeen real, boyhood days we had to wait until Christmas finally came.

I was much older before I realized that my childish waiting was only an absurd little parable of the real wait our world has known. Charles Wesley has a term for it in one of the hymns churches and choirs sing during this season: "Come, thou long-expected Jesus."

When Charles Wesley says of the Christmas story that it was "long-expected," how long did he mean? How long has the human race waited for Christmas? As long, it seems to me, as it has perceived anything of truth, reality, and hope; as long as it has had any longing beyond a hand that reaches for food. As long as there has been a human race, there has been a longing for Christmas. "Come, thou long-expected Jesus"!

The most powerful description of our longing comes to us from the Jewish people in the books of the Old Testament. The Jews were expecting. One of the most poignant statements is found in the prophet Isaiah:

> The people who walked in darkness
>   have seen a great light;
> those who dwelt in a land of deep darkness,
>   on them has light shined. (Isaiah 9:2)

I suppose there is hardly a Christian church in the world where these verses will not be read, sung, or preached sometime during these weeks leading up to Christmas. Many a secular person, with little regard for the divine significance of Jesus, will nevertheless sing this passage as part of some oratorio choir or chorus.

I am enough of a sentimentalist to enjoy all the trappings that have grown up around this season. I can find pleasure in Rudolph, the Red-Nosed Reindeer; the prospect of seeing Mommy kissing Santa Claus; and chestnuts roasting on an open fire. The tunes and lyrics of these songs touch the springs of nostalgia; and because those springs of nostalgia lie so close to some misty longings of our human hearts, they usually refresh some sense of warmth and wonder.

But God forbid that we should stop there. In truth, we aren't able to stop there, even if we want to. It's no wonder that the Christmas season leaves so many feeling depressed and let down. If our focus is too largely on the chestnuts of the open fire, too much on presents and parties, too much even on friends and family, we will prospect at last in an empty vein. Christmas is more than all of these. It is a celebration of the coming of the Savior of the earth, the One who has power to set us free from our fears and sins, and to give us rest in this world and in the world to come.

He is, indeed, the "long-expected Jesus." It is not only that the human race has awaited him from its most ancient times and that peoples have anticipated him without knowing his name and without understanding his origins. It is that each of us, you and I, has our own personal longing.

So if I were to ask you, as we approach the Christmas season, "How long have you waited for Christmas?" or in more common and direct language, "How long have you been looking for help, real help?" I would receive specific answers. Someone would say, "I've been waiting since my marriage failed," and the person who says it might still be in the midst of that marriage. And another would say, "I've been waiting since my girlfriend dumped me." Still another would report, "I've been waiting since my mother died"; and another, "I've been waiting since shortly after I finished high school, when some of my dreams began to fall flat." And someone with a poetic, philosophical bent might answer, "How long have I been waiting? Ever since I was born."

And so have we all. We are the human race, so touched with divinity that we cannot long be satisfied with mistletoe and chestnuts, with parties and reunions, with sentiment and the sound of music. There is a longing deep in our souls that is as old as eternity, and nothing short of the touch of the Eternal One will meet it.

How long have you been waiting for Christmas? "For months," a little boy says. "Ever since last Christmas," a little girl answers. But the prophets of Israel, the writers of the Scriptures, the thoughtful and articulate peoples of the earth will answer, "Longer than that, much longer. The earth was waiting for him from its foundations, and the human race from its first whole breath. And each of us, individually, has waited alone since first we began to feel the truth of beauty, love, and honor."

He is the long-expected Jesus. Let us make our hearts ready for a new meeting with him.

December 3

Crowded Inn, Crowded Life

*I*n this season, when so many of us seem to have more to do than time in which to do it—this season that we call "the Christmas rush," when for many the most popular theme is not "peace on earth, goodwill," but rather, "I don't know if I can possibly get everything finished in time for the holidays"—at such a time as this, we do well to consider a man long ago who had the same problem. I think I might call him the patron saint of crowded lives. I don't know that he ever became a saint, but that makes the title all the more appropriate; for it's very hard for any of us to achieve saintliness when our lives get too crowded.

Thousands of poems, stories, plays, and dramatic skits have been written about this man, yet we don't even know his name. In fact, we don't really know anything about him, except that his life was crowded. Well, perhaps it wasn't always crowded; but on the night when he made his unique contribution to human history, it was crowded to the point of crisis. He was an innkeeper.

His wasn't a very impressive hotel. Some years ago, while leading a tour group in the Holy Land, I stopped for refreshments in an inn in Jordan that I was told may be the oldest in the world. Even with modern lighting and an attempt to appeal to tourists, it was a pretty gloomy spot, so I can imagine what a typical, small-town hotel was like in the first century. Writer A. C. Bouquet says that it was no doubt "dirty, badly kept, badly managed, with leaky roofs, and generally uncomfortable." Inns in the ancient world were often centers of criminal and immoral activities. Government officials and soldiers on the march could claim free lodging, which must have forced innkeepers to charge more from private travelers to make up the loss.[1]

It was a busy season, perhaps the busiest Bethlehem had known since anyone could remember. Caesar Augustus had passed a new tax law, which required that people return to their ancestral homes to register for the taxation. That thrust hundreds of travelers out on the highways. A good number of them stopped at the hotel in Bethlehem, either en route to a destination down the road or—like a young carpenter named Joseph—because Bethlehem was their registration city.

So the innkeeper was very busy. It was both frustrating and exciting. Several times he must have muttered to a servant that it would be nice if some of this business could be spread out over the slow season. I am sure he hurried about, checking on supplies of fuel and food, answering questions from confused travelers, and hurrying along an irresponsible employee. Perhaps he hardly noticed Joseph and Mary, the travelers from Nazareth, when they came seeking a room.

As a matter of fact, maybe he didn't even deal with them personally. Poet Amos Russel Wells imagines the innkeeper explaining afterward, "I saw them not myself, my servants must have driven them away."[2] Perhaps it was that way. Since the inn was already full, it could be that the innkeeper had retired for the evening and had left a servant or a slave at the door to turn away latecomers. Maybe he had just hung out a No Vacancy sign. But even if the innkeeper handled the matter personally, you can't blame him too much; or at the very least, you can understand his predicament.

You see, we ought to understand the innkeeper very well. He was not a villainous man, as far as we can tell from this story. It's just that he was so busy. And we understand busyness—the student who has three term papers due tomorrow and a final exam in the afternoon; the employee who is swamped at work, dealing with unexpected interruptions, and pressured by deadlines; the family who is juggling schedules, preparing for guests, and trying to do right by the seasonal decorating and shopping. We understand busyness. We understand the innkeeper.

Indeed, the innkeeper's problem was that he was so successful that night, he didn't have any more room. And that's the way it is with so many of us.

You and I have so many things going at once. We have so many obligations and opportunities at work, at home, at school, in the community, and in society that we really haven't any room for Christ. We bear him no ill will. In fact, in most instances we hardly realize that he is seeking entrance. We're so preoccupied that we hear no knock, no request for recognition. Perhaps, in a manner of speaking, we have sent a servant to answer the door, and we do not know that we have rejected the King.

I'm just trying to say that the innkeeper wasn't necessarily a bad person; no worse than the majority of us, probably. He bore no malice against Joseph and Mary. It's just that his life was crowded. And that's the point of the matter. One doesn't have to hate Christ in order to shut him out. All it takes to exclude him is to be crowded—filled up—with no available room.

I Believe in Christmas

I believe in Christmas. Mind you, believing is not always easy. Sometimes, the un-Christmas-like nature of my own heart makes it hard for me to believe in Christmas. We are that way. We are unable, sometimes, to believe in goodness because of our own lack of goodness. Sometimes we think that all people lie because we have lied; and just so, sometimes we cannot believe in Christmas because we have so little of Christmas in our own hearts.

But even when one's heart is full of goodwill, it can sometimes be hard to believe in Christmas. Christmas, as with all good things, can be smothered easily by the paraphernalia that accumulates around it. This happens to weddings, graduations, baptisms, and confirmations. But Christmas suffers worst of all.

Christmas is so easily exploited, or misunderstood, or misused. We set out to give gifts to those we love and to those who seem to us to be in need; but before long the giving gets twisted out of shape— we give because we know another is going to give to us, and we feel we must balance their action; or we give because we feel obligated; or we give for business or professional reasons. Surely much of the Christmas giving has become badly perverted; it not only misses the purpose of Christmas, but it twists that purpose all out of shape.

The Gospel writer said, long ago, that Jesus Christ had come into the world as a light, and that the darkness had never been able to overcome that light (John 1:4-5). I think the same word can be applied to the Christmas spirit: this spirit of Christmas that has come into the world has been misused, perverted, and exploited, smothered under the paraphernalia that accompanies it—yet nothing has ever been able to overcome it.

Most of us have heard the Christmas stories from World War I. At times during that war, the opposing lines were entrenched within calling distance of each other; and in several instances, according to reports, the men who were obligated through the rest of the year to kill one another chose on Christmas Day to eat, sing, and play together. Even war cannot overcome the spirit of Christmas.

What is true on the vast stage of the world is true also on the modest stage of our private lives. We reach out in ways at Christmas that perhaps we don't the rest of the year. We do things for other people. We think about it at other times, but at Christmas we turn the thought into the act.

We give at Christmastime, too. In the midst of the giving that is perfunctory, by obligation, or for "business reasons," nearly everyone does some special giving. Sometimes it is no more than the money dropped into the kettle of the street corner Santa, and sometimes it is a gift for someone who has less than you; but even the most mercenary come to feel at this season that they ought to give something

for the sheer joy of giving. The age in which we live may be materialistic, but even materialism has not been able to overcome the spirit of
Christmas.

In fact, nothing can overcome the spirit of Christmas, because
Christmas is built on a fact. Part of the fact is written into human history; the other part is written into the human heart. On the side of
human history, a child was born in the city of Bethlehem, in the days
of Caesar Augustus. The Christian religion claims proudly to be a historical religion, based not on myth or fantasy but on a real event in an
identifiable period of recorded history.

But the fact of Christmas is more than human history; more
important, it is something that has been written on the human
heart. We believe the Christmas story because we cannot escape it.
Intellectually, some will balk at elements of the Christmas story, but
they cannot write it off emotionally. Below the story of shepherds and
angels, wise men and a star, is a ground of truth that cannot be moved.
It withstands the worst in us. We fight wars, and we build walls against
our neighbors, yet Christmas is not overcome. We bury Christmas
under our bustling commercialism and our misguided celebrations,
yet Christmas rises again. When one considers how Christmas has
withstood the opposition of its enemies and the ineptitude of its
friends for more than twenty centuries, and how still today it touches
even the meanest of people, one is left with a dilemma for the doubter:
how to explain the Christmas spirit.

Perhaps it is not surprising that every generation builds its
myths around the Christmas story. Other generations have had their
Christmas tree and their yule log, their kneeling animals and their
King Wenceslas; our generation has its misguided office parties and

commercialized exploitation of giving—and perhaps it could not be otherwise. That is, perhaps we cannot help but surround Christmas with sentiment and mystery and our own brand of legend; for otherwise, Christmas is too big to grasp. We dress Christmas in cloth that is sometimes shoddy and sometimes grotesque because we are looking for a garment large enough and grand enough to encompass what is beyond our ken.

So I believe in Christmas. I believe there was an event in an obscure village more than twenty centuries ago that was God's gift to the world. I believe that the spirit of that event not only touches the lives of those who believe in it but also seems each Christmas to be inescapable even to many who deny and deride it. I believe that God so loved the world that he gave his Son (John 3:16). I believe that God's gift is unconquerable; thus, human beings can never overcome the spirit of Christmas.

I believe in Christmas.

December 5

Three Wise Shoppers

I don't have to tell you that Christmas is a shopping season; you know it. In fact, you may feel you know it all too well. Some people even say that Christmas shopping and giving have become entirely pagan. They point to the extravagance of much of the giving and the exploitation of Christmas by some merchants, and they insist that it has ceased to be a truly Christian celebration.

But on the other hand, that's up to us. I think there's some justification for the businessman who wrote some years ago, "Gift-giving at Christmas is not secular unless we permit it to be so. It's up to the merchant to provide us with a selection for our gift buying. It's up to us to supply the proper motive for the giving."[1]

That brings us to those original Christmas shoppers: the three wise men. The Bible doesn't really tell us much about them. In fact, we don't even know for sure that there were three. We speak of three because three gifts were presented, but the Bible doesn't give us a number. It simply reports that "wise men from the East came to

Jerusalem, saying, 'Where is he who has been born king of the Jews? For we have seen his star in the East, and have come to worship him'" (Matthew 2:1b-2). When at last they found him, they presented their gifts: gold, frankincense, and myrrh; then they went home by another way, in order to protect the Child's life. This is all the Bible tells us, for only Matthew's Gospel records the wise men's visit.

I want to talk to you about the wise men as the first Christmas shoppers—the three wise shoppers. Are you offended that I call them "three wise shoppers"? Does that phrase seem a little flippant or irreverent? I don't mean it to be so. I mean it as a compliment. After all, the wise men gave the first Christmas gifts and have been honored for centuries for the beauty and appropriateness of their gifts. How could they have found such excellent and appropriate gifts if they were not good shoppers? A selection such as theirs did not happen by chance. They must have worked very hard at it.

Do not let *Christmas shopping* become a nasty phrase. Giving isn't bad; and how can you give without shopping? *Shopping*, in fact, ought to be a word that implies thought. Perhaps the most important step in shopping occurs within, as you think through the persons you intend to favor and ponder what will please and benefit them the most. It takes effort to find the right gift. If shopping were only a matter of money, it would be much simpler than it is. With more money we can buy more expensive gifts, but not necessarily more appropriate ones.

The men who gave the first Christmas gifts were wise shoppers. They didn't really know anything about the Child for whom they were shopping, except that he was born to be a king. Now what do you buy for a child who is to become a king? Did these wise shoppers wander for hours and days in the bazaars and shops of the Middle East? Did they look at item after item, examining quality and inquiring about the artisans? I think they did. I think they must have shopped long and earnestly. And did they perhaps become victims of shoppers' fatigue, until they said, "I don't think we'll ever find anything that's just right!" Perhaps so. The fact that they were working on a grand and divine mission doesn't mean they were relieved of all human reactions.

But at last their quest was complete: gold, frankincense, and myrrh. Theologians find symbolism in each gift. Gold was the traditional royal gift, thus it was a recognition of Christ as king. Frankincense was the special property of the priest in the act of worship, thus honoring Christ's role as the eternal high priest of all who accept him. Myrrh was used to embalm the bodies of the dead, which reminds us that Jesus came to die for our sins. Thus, the gold, frankincense, and myrrh describe Jesus Christ as king, priest, and Savior.

Do you suppose the wise men wondered, when they came to a stable, if they had made a mistake? Did they look at their expensive, regal gifts—then look at the ugly stable—and question whether they had made the wrong choice of gifts? Whatever their questions may have been, they gave their gifts: the magnificent gold, frankincense, and myrrh.

And that tells us that these wise shoppers were men of great faith. We often miss that point, don't we? We know they were men of wisdom, wealth, and even of reverent love; but have you paused to realize that they were men of exceeding faith? They believed so deeply that they could see beyond the humble setting and make their gift of love and substance.

Three wise shoppers! The wise men had to buy their gifts in a shopping center, too, you know. Yet in the midst of the commerce and the hustle, the wise men held onto love and faith; such love and faith that even a mean stable or a peasant hut could not disturb them. They looked at a baby and saw a King. And they gave him gifts for a king.

We don't need to put an end to Christmas shopping and giving. But we need more wise shoppers, who will go about the business of Christmas as if they really expect that it will all climax in Bethlehem, at the throne of a Savior-King.

December 6

Christmas Word: Troubled

We think of Christmas customarily in the language of joy. The verb that we always associate with Christmas is *celebrate*— we celebrate Christmas. The native sound of Christmas is music and bells, and the quality of Christmas is laughter. So it seems incongruous to include *troubled* in the vocabulary of Christmas, doesn't it?

Yet when we read the story of the first Christmas, we come on the word *troubled* (Matthew 2:3). It is an inevitable part of the language of that first Christmas, as surely a part of the mood as was the adoration of the wise men and the joy of the shepherds. But perhaps the reason that our modern Christmas is not as deeply and radically happy as it ought to be is because we have tried to make it too superficially happy. We have wanted Christmas to be a season of unadulterated joy. But Christmas isn't like that, really. Christmas is joy following a crisis. It is joy after troubling.

The first Christmas was a troubled time for one key personality in the Christmas story, and for all those associated with him.

He was a king; the Bible calls him Herod. He was a quite successful king, possessed of some of the skills that would have qualified him in Machiavelli's eyes. He rose to power at a time of civil war and internal strife. He had to please Caesar if he wanted to remain in Rome's good graces, but he had also to maintain a degree of peace in the segment of the empire that was under his control. He managed to walk that tightrope in effective fashion; and although it was at a high price, he was able to gain a good degree of order and peace.

Just when it appeared that he had his kingdom comfortably under control, three wise men from the East appeared in Jerusalem. They were looking for a king, they said, a baby born to be king of the Jews. Apparently they were astrologers of a kind, for they said that they had seen a star in the East, the star of the new king, and that they had come now to worship him. "When Herod the king heard this," the reporter writes, "he was troubled, and all Jerusalem with him."

At first it seems strange to the point of being absurd. Why should a king be frightened at the birth of a child? But on second thought, it isn't so surprising that the king was troubled—nor is his response to life so different from our own. So many people in high positions are insecure. Herod was typical of his kind. He was king, and he wanted to remain king; now someone had appeared on the scene, according to rumor, who appeared to be a competitor for his crown.

So many people work and plan, scramble and claw, to get a position, then live in fear day after day that someone will take it from them. There are Herods on every sports team, in every fraternity and sorority, in every business, and in the heart of the social world—"kings" and "queens" who wonder when someone will come along and unseat them.

In fact, there's a little of the king or queen in all of us—and there ought to be. Each of us is entrusted with a kingdom, the governing of our own lives. So we're sensitive about our little kingdom. "I'm my own boss," we say. "No one tells me what to do." We're jealous of our rulership. "I've got my rights!" Without this sense of our own worth, and of our innate rights, we would cease to be human. The despots and dictators of human history have run into their most formidable enemy at just this point. But we each have some sense of our own right to govern our life or to have a voice in its governing.

And that's why *troubled* is a right word for the vocabulary of Christmas. If you read the Christmas story carefully, you'll feel some kinship with Herod. Suddenly he is not just a vicious, Machiavellian despot who murders little babies; he is someone like you, a person whose throne is threatened by the Christmas babe. For when the Christmas bells ring, they announce the birth of a King; and if he is a King who brings joy to the world, he is also a King who asks for a throne. And the throne is the one you'd like to have.

Christmas ought to trouble us. If we read it correctly, it will trouble us in order to bless us and prior to blessing us. For the Christmas story says that God is concerned about us; but that's a message that is as frightening as it is comforting. When the Christmas story says that love came down at Christmas, it is half blessing and half demand. Christ is always the claimant to the throne of our lives. This, after all, is what the Christian faith means when it calls him *Lord*. This he was born to be, and with this claim he troubles us. He comes to claim a throne, and the throne is the human heart.

"When Herod the king heard . . . he was troubled." Indeed! Jesus Christ troubles me, too. I set up a pattern of life, thinking I've got it made; then one day, wise men come round and I hear there is another King. My wise men don't come from the East; they seem built into the fabric of my life. They remind me that I am not ruling well, that a new king is needed.

And a voice quietly asks me, "Who is king around here?"

Christmas Creed: Conceived by the Holy Spirit

*W*e are involved in a controversial story. Surely it must have been a controversial subject in the village of Nazareth nineteen centuries ago when a girl named Mary was found to be with child. It continues to be a controversial subject in our day.

The controversy is summed up in two phrases of the Apostles' Creed, the phrases that describe Jesus Christ in this fashion: "who was conceived by the Holy Spirit, born of the Virgin Mary." In one sense, the two phrases are inseparable; but in another way, the two phrases emphasize different aspects of the same story. I am choosing therefore to discuss theology when I talk about the phrase "conceived by the Holy Spirit."

One of the key phrases in the Christmas story is the term *the virgin birth*. No doubt about it, the virgin birth is a difficult doctrine.

Traditionally, the Christian church has not compelled its believers to accept the virgin birth in a physical, literal sense; it has allowed them to accept it literally or figuratively. Only two of the four Gospels, Matthew and Luke, give us the story of Christ's birth. Both of them emphasize that Jesus was conceived by the Spirit of God and born of the virgin.

I don't believe that the virgin birth is a foundation stone of the Christian faith. It is not, in that respect, like the resurrection of Christ. The first Christian sermons, as recorded in the Book of Acts, indicated that the faith would stand or fall on the issue of the resurrection; but they make no reference to the virgin birth. The apostle Paul makes no clear reference to it in all of his writings. It seems likely, therefore, that in the early Christian church, the virgin birth was not a matter that was emphasized in the way some other doctrines are emphasized, and it doesn't seem likely that people were required to believe in the virgin birth in order to be members of the Christian church.

But even if it was not a required teaching in the early Christian church, it was surely a part of their belief. Since both Matthew and Luke include the virgin birth in their account, it can surely be assumed that this was part of the story as customarily understood in the first century.

How shall we judge the historical accuracy of Matthew and Luke? First of all, we must confess that they were closer to the facts than we are. That is, they were in a position to know what was commonly believed in the early church, since they were part of it. Furthermore, we probably ought to remember that Luke was a doctor; and while very much a child of his time, he was no doubt more critical of birth accounts than a layperson would be. Yet Luke gives us the story of a miraculous birth.

But the bigger question remains: What did the New Testament writers mean by the story of the virgin birth? Whether you accept the story literally or figuratively, it is not an end in itself. If Jesus was born by miraculous, extraordinary means, there must have been some significance in the peculiar means; and if the story is meant only to be symbolical, then we ought to seek out the meaning of the symbols. What is meant by this remarkable and mysterious story, this story of a peasant girl who hears an angel voice telling her that she is to have a baby and that the baby has been conceived by the Spirit of God?

A number of centuries before Christmas, a man in deep trouble—Job—uttered a pathetic complaint:

> For [God] is not a man, as I am, that I might answer him,
> > that we should come to trial together.
> There is no umpire between us,
> > who might lay his hand upon us both. (Job 9:32-33)

An "umpire" is precisely what we needed: someone who could lay hands upon us both. That is, we needed someone who could lay a hand on God and a hand on humanity. But who, in all this creation, could touch us both?

Obviously, it was a situation where God would have to take the initiative. Humanity could never make the reach to heaven, but perhaps God could make the descent to earth. And so the Christmas story begins, not with the virgin Mary but with the Holy Spirit. The term *virgin birth* is not really a satisfactory phrase. What I mean is this: the emphasis is at the wrong point. The Christmas story does not begin with Mary; it begins with God. The Mary who is willing to be used of the Lord is not the starting point but the God who seeks her out. The Apostles' Creed is right when it makes God the initiator of the action: he "was conceived by the Holy Spirit." In the redemption of humanity, God is the aggressor.

Here is what the Christmas story is saying: God so loved the world, that he came into the world, so that we might enter the kingdom of heaven. I think that you can believe that God came into the world in Jesus Christ whether you accept the virgin birth literally or figuratively. How do I believe? Let me be as honest as I know how. I don't disbelieve the literal story. If the first Christians meant the story literally, I will accept their testimony as reliable witnesses, realizing that they were twenty centuries closer to the scene of action than I. I'm not sure that they meant it literally; but if they did, I am able to accept their witness.

Far more important, I believe what the birth is trying to say: I believe that humanity needed an "umpire," someone who could lay a hand on us and a hand on God. I believe that if such a go-between were to be found, who could touch both God and humanity, it would have to be an action initiated by God. I believe that God took precisely such an action at Christmas: that the way of salvation was conceived by God.

I believe, that is, that Jesus Christ was "conceived by the Holy Spirit"; and that because he was so conceived, we may be born again as children of God.

December 8

That Blessed Comma

I want to talk with you about a frequently misplaced comma. That's right, a comma.

Right near the top of my list of favorite Christmas carols is that wonderfully rambunctious English number from the eighteenth century, "God Rest You Merry, Gentlemen." Quite often someone says, "How come a fellow like you is so in love with that song? Those merry gentlemen sound like a group of fellows well into their cups."

That's where the comma is an issue. I find that some secular books of Christmas songs—the kind often given out generously by business establishments—put the comma in the wrong place, making the song read, "God Rest You, Merry Gentlemen." Now with that approach, it might sound like a drinking song or a fraternity song. But the correct place for the comma is after the "Merry," so that it reads, "God Rest You Merry, Gentlemen"—that is, God make your rest happy and joyful . . . merry as only the true Christmas can make it.

Now if this were only a matter of grammar, it would hardly be worth mentioning. But it has to do with the whole mixed-up attitude people have toward Christmas. When you think of all the Christmas parties, dinners, receptions, and celebrations that never give a thought to the Christ Child, you realize how many people are putting the comma in the wrong place. They think that Christmas is for merry gentlemen, so to speak; that is, an occasion made significant by food, beverages, festivities, and all such.

But it is God who brings the "merry," the happy, into Christmas. You can't drink enough, eat enough, spend enough, or party enough to make Christmas merry, especially when it is time to "rest" and ponder it all. The "merry" comes when our hearts bow low at Bethlehem . . . when we honor Jesus Christ as Lord and King.

Mind you, I have nothing against Christmas celebrations. I like them very much.

But they are after the fact. They do something for us only if we've involved ourselves in the greater business of Christmas.

It reminds me of that old Mother Goose rhyme:

> "Pussy-cat, pussy-cat,
> Where have you been?"
> "I've been to London
> To look at the Queen."
>
> "Pussy cat, pussy cat,
> What did you there?"
> "I frightened a little mouse
> Under the chair."

What a silly pussy cat! After going all the way to London to visit the queen, she spent her time doing something she could have done just as well at home: frightening a little mouse under the chair.

And that's what people do with Christmas when they put the comma in the wrong place. They come to this best of all seasons, when they might meet with God and fall in love anew with the human race, and they spend it trying to be "merry gentlemen." They could do that sort of thing any other season of the year. But Christmas is special: it's a time for coming to the palace of the King, and it's a shame at such a time and place to waste oneself in chasing mice.

So that's the story of the blessed comma. Keep it in the right place. If you try to find Christmas in merry celebrations and merry fellows, you'll end the season with loneliness, hangover, and depression. If you really want to celebrate Christmas, you must come to God, for he makes merry.

Rejoice, then, as the last verse of that lively carol does:

> Now to the Lord sing praises,
> All you within this place,
> And with true love and brotherhood
> Each other now embrace;
> This holy tide of Christmas
> All others doth deface.
> O tidings of comfort and joy, comfort and joy;
> O tidings of comfort and joy.

December 9

Christmas Word: Sin

A devotional for Advent, the season in which we prepare ourselves for Christmas, ought to be a gentle, lovely thing. So I can understand the uneasiness you may feel when you see that my topic for the day is sin. How can sin be thought of as one of the Christmas words? In the same way, I expect, that *disease* is classified as a medical word, or *hunger* as a culinary word, or *loneliness* as a romantic word. For you see, the Christmas story begins not with lights and gifts, not with parties and greeting cards, not even with an angel chorus and a manger in which a baby lies sleeping, but with human need. And the name of the human need is sin.

Our Christmas music tells us this again and again, but the words are so familiar and the music so lilting that we hardly hear what we're singing. We sing with Charles Wesley,

> Come, thou long-expected Jesus,
> born to set thy people free;

from our fears and sins release us,
let us find our rest in thee.[1]

And then, in one of the most rollicking and glad songs of the season, "Joy to the World," we sing,

No more let sins and sorrows grow,
nor thorns infest the ground;
he comes to make his blessings flow
far as the curse is found.[2]

The Christmas story begins with sin, with human need. If there were not such a thing as sin, there would be no need for Christmas, just as there would be no need for healing if there was not such a thing as sickness.

It is no doubt significant that sin appears so early in the human story. The human skin doesn't yet have its first wrinkle of age when sin shows itself. When the psalmist says he was conceived in sin and brought forth in iniquity, he isn't condemning sexual union; he's trying to tell us that sin is a problem of human life from before the time we are born, that it is with us always. This story from Genesis underlines that idea: our human history, from the very beginning, is woven through with the fact of sin.

No book looks at sin so starkly and realistically as does the Bible, yet no book is so compassionate in the language it uses to describe sin. *Disobedience* and *rebellion* are the hardest words; most of the others emphasize the pathetic nature of our human plight.

The word the Bible uses most often is one that means literally "to miss the mark." For ancient peoples this word described an archer who aimed at a target and missed. This is sin, to have had our aim at life go astray, to miss the mark. This is a man in jail saying, "I never thought my life would end up here." This is someone looking back on a life that seems terribly wasted and crying, "I don't know how this happened to me. I don't know how I missed the mark so badly."

The Jewish understanding of sin, especially in the Yom Kippur services, carries this idea still further when it emphasizes "losing sight of the important things in life." Sin is not simply the grossness, the brutality, the inhumanity that we usually picture; it is losing sight of those things in life that are supremely important while we pursue that which is petty or inconsequential.

Another Old Testament word speaks of sin as "going astray." A sinner is someone who has left the main road of life. Life is meant to lead to a sure and purposeful goal. When we sin, we make it into a stumbling wilderness. Or worse yet, we become like a traveler who is racing down the highway at full speed, never realizing his car is headed in the wrong direction.

The apostle Paul speaks in this same mood when he says that all sin and "fall short" of the glory of God (Romans 3:23). The Greek word for "fall short" is actually a word that means "be destitute" or "be in want." It is the sage word that Jesus used to describe the condition of the prodigal in the far country: he began to be in want, to be destitute. Sin is the ultimate poverty; it is the human soul struggling with a debt it can never pay.

And sin is more than simply the deed I do, the thought I think, the word I speak. It is so much a part of the world in which I live that

I almost breathe it in the very process of living. Sin surrounds me in the forms of fear, despair, loneliness, doubt. Though I may not want to give in to these things, they attack me when I'm not looking.

But then I think again of "Joy to the World": "He comes to make his blessings flow / far as the curse is found." I would not preach about sin if I could not tell you about the Savior.

Christmas is God's answer to the tragedy called sin. Sin is like an incurable illness that afflicts our human race, and Christmas gives us the Great Physician. Sin has made us bankrupt, but Jesus the Christ paid the debt we cannot pay. We have wandered astray, and Christmas means that God has gone searching for us. However great and pervasive the curse of sin may be, "He comes to make his blessings flow far as the curse is found."

And so we celebrate this season. For when we face the overpowering, incurable word *sin*, God has answered with bigger words: *Jesus Christ*. Christmas has come to make us victors over sin.

December 10

Christmas Word: Grace

*Y*esterday we examined the word *sin*. But there is another word found more frequently in the Bible than sin, even though sin can be used as both a noun and a verb. In fact, today's word is one of the words found most often: grace. The word *grace* appears some 130 times in the New Testament.

Still more important is the way in which grace is used. It is so often the blessing and benediction word of the New Testament. When you read it you can almost see outstretched hands and widespread arms. The thirteen New Testament books that are commonly referred to as the Letters of Paul—beginning with Romans and ending with Philemon—all have grace as part of their greeting and as their closing blessing. Paul greeted people by praying the grace of God upon them, and he said farewell with the same blessing.

In fact, this is rather interesting: each of these letters has as its greeting some form of the sentence "Grace to you, and peace." But as a conclusion, in almost every sentence only grace is used: "Grace be with you," or, "The grace of our Lord Jesus Christ be with you." In our day the word *peace* has again become a popular word of greeting and farewell. It is an appropriate, beautiful practice. I think it might be even better, however, if we revived the word *grace*. For I have a strong feeling we won't get much peace until we experience more grace.

In the New Testament the Greek word for grace is *charis*, which means "sheer, undeserved generosity." In its simplest form it means gift: something a person never deserves and could never earn. Ancient Greeks used the word to describe beauty and charm. They might use it while viewing a sunset, or a delicate flower, or a lovely human face. In its original form it meant beauty. As Christians used it more and more, it came especially to mean divine beauty, a gift of God's generous love and goodness. *Grace* is a word that was obviously very dear to the first generations of Christians. It made their hearts leap with joy and hope and gratitude to hear "Grace to you!"

From the divine side, perhaps there is no single word that is closer to the heart of the Christian faith than this word *grace*. Grace means that God accepts us out of his kindness, and that our deserving has nothing to do with it. That idea offends our self-respect. Popular religion says, "You do the best you can, and you'll make it." But Christianity replies, "You do the best you can, and you'll still be a thousand miles short of the goal." If we are ever to have a right relationship with God, it will be because of God's grace, his "sheer, undeserved generosity," which bridges the gap between God and our inadequate best.

Grace is strategically important to us because we are confronted with a debt we cannot pay. When we argue that we can make the grade simply by doing the best we can, we give evidence that we simply don't understand the predicament we're in. Our sin is not simply a sin against the law. If it were, we could make it right: we would give so many dollars to church and charity or perhaps serve a period of time in some sacrificial labor. But our sin is against the love of God, and how does one make that right? We cannot; the only thing that can right our relationship with God is for God to forgive us. That's why we must have grace. We haven't a chance for a clearing of the slate except by grace: "sheer, undeserved generosity."

And that's the meaning of the Christmas story. Saint Paul wrote, "For you know the grace of our Lord Jesus Christ, that though he was rich, yet for your sake he became poor, so that by his poverty you might become rich" (2 Corinthians 8:9). Grace is spelled out at Bethlehem: the Son of God divests himself of the riches of his divinity and takes on the poverty of our humanity, so that through his giving we might receive the eternal wealth of the sons and daughters of God.

In other words, grace is a very special word for the love of God. It is love at its outer limits. Love sometimes has its reasons, but grace has no reasons. Love sometimes makes sense, but grace makes no sense. The essence of grace is that it loves contrary to reason. Alexander Maclaren once said that "grace is love that stoops."[1] It stoops down to our need, reaches out to our lostness, is not repelled by our arrogance, and pursues us to the limits.

Grace is a gift: "sheer, undeserved generosity." We human beings were in a predicament. We had broken not simply the law of God but the heart of God. Condemnation was upon us.

So we prepared ourselves for Judgment Day. But when we awakened, it was Christmas morning.

That is grace.

December 11

Heaven's Invader

*E*very baby is a mystery of expectation. If we are in any measure poetic or philosophic, we wonder, as we look at a newborn child, if perhaps the baby will become some benefactor of the human race. In this seven- or eight-pound conglomerate you may have a president, a poet, a teacher, an executive, a quarterback, a novelist, or a saint. And then again, you may have a drug addict, a pimp, a demagogue, or a murderer. In that little package—so helpless that if you leave it untended for a relatively short time it will die—there is unlimited mystery.

And if that is true of any baby, how much more is it true of the baby born in Bethlehem? Prophets had anticipated the birth of one who would deliver, and sages of many cultures had predicted a day when peace and righteousness would cover the earth. And then there came a baby to a stable in back of Bethlehem's one hotel. Shepherds bowed and wise men left their gifts. Now, baby, what are you going to be?

Among the many things he was to be, he was heaven's invader. He came to earth because our planet had been taken hostage by an alien force. He came as Deliverer to restore our planet and its inhabitants to our rightful freedom.

You will find this story in the first chapter of the Gospel of John. Where Matthew and Luke tell us of Christmas with scenes in Nazareth, Jerusalem, and Bethlehem, John's Gospel takes us into the starry reaches before the measure of time, and into the mind of Almighty God. John says, "In the beginning was the Word, and the Word was with God, and the Word was God" (v. 1). And then John moves the scene to earth. He refers to Jesus as "the true light that enlightens every man . . . coming into the world," and says, "He was in the world, and the world was made through him, yet the world knew him not. He came to his own home, and his own people received him not. . . . And the Word became flesh and dwelt among us, full of grace and truth" (John 1:1, 9-11, 14a).

The Creator brought into being a vast universe. He gave one of the planets special significance by making it particularly (perhaps uniquely) hospitable to life. He peopled it with a race of creatures that we call human beings. These human beings are a special breed, indeed. A dog is a dog, and a rose is a rose; but a human being—he or she can be divine or demonic, lovely or hateful, heavenly or hellish—or an infinite variety of gradations between. And this human being alone, among all the creatures of the planet, can decide whether or not he or she will cooperate with the Creator. Other elements of the creation do what comes naturally. You and I decide what we will do. We decide whether we will fulfill the will of the Creator or whether we will go our independent and rebellious ways.

We heard an alien voice, and the voice was often so attractive that we believed it. The voice said, in a variety of ways, "Don't pay attention to that old fogy Creator. Do your own thing! He's trying to frustrate you by all sorts of rules and limitations. Don't let Him fence you in." Now mind you, our planet and its inhabitants have never fully believed those lies, but we've believed them often enough that the planet is in rebellion.

So the Creator said, "We have to bring it back into holy, purposeful orbit." But how is that to be done? What do you do with a planet in rebellion? The answer: mount an invasion. Invade the planet and restore it.

How do you go about invading a planet? The logical approach, to our human minds, is to send some armed body; indeed, a massive, powerful armed body. Smash the opposing power and bring it under submission. That's the customary style of invasion.

But that isn't the way the Creator did it. Because what the Creator wants from this planet and its inhabitants is not beaten submissiveness but willing discipleship. The Creator seeks our love, not our terror. So he invaded the planet in the most helpless, disarming fashion. He sent a baby.

More than twenty centuries later, the struggle still goes on, and the invasion still continues. It is an invasion, not directly of culture or of governments, but of individual human lives. He seeks to become Lord of our hearts. He comes to the world of which, by creation and right, he is Lord, and begs admittance; the humility of the Christ is beyond comprehension. And we decide whether or not we will let him in.

Christ keeps mounting his offensive. During the dark hour of loneliness, in our time of disappointment, in an instance where we see the futility of our prized accomplishment, he chips away at our defenses. He comes always in love, and never will he take control unless, willingly, we welcome him. For while he is committed to becoming your Lord and mine, he will not force his way in. His is a lordship that is effective only by our willing acceptance. Ultimately, his invasion can happen only when we choose to surrender. He is Lord by right, but he will become your Lord and mine only if we say yes to him.

"Give me the throne," he pleads, "so your little personal planet will run rightly. Give me your troubles, your fears, your failures; and also your pride, your success, and your power—and let Me reign. I fit your throne, and you do not. Give me the place that will set your little planet in order."

He came to be Heaven's Invader. Let us, today, surrender to him.

December 12

The Weak Power

The weakness of Christmas is plain to see. The whole story seems to be an exercise in weakness. After all, it centers around a baby, and what could be more helpless and vulnerable than a human baby? What an unlikely invader to send to a world so badly in need of reform.

And consider where the baby was born. He was born not in a seat of power—not a king's palace nor even a scholar's study—but in a cave-barn. The baby was born to common folk, an apprentice carpenter and his teenage bride.

And no doubt the baby was born in some disrepute. It is not only that his parents were poor and temporarily disestablished, but some of the village gossips in Nazareth probably raised questions about their character and conduct. And for that matter, it was disreputable enough just to live in the village of Nazareth. In those days people said, "Can anything good come out of Nazareth?" (John 1:46). It was that kind of town. Jesus did not enjoy the prestige of coming from

Rome or Athens or Jerusalem. He suffered the weakness of coming from Nazareth.

I'm sure that the first-century world was not looking for such weakness. The Jews badly needed a leader, but this was not the kind of leader they sought. Several times in prior years men had appeared on the scene who promised military victory and revolution, and thousands flocked after them. But the Jews weren't looking for a baby in a manger, because that was weakness.

And surely the Gentile world had no such leader in mind. The Romans paid homage to a vast military machine and to administrative power. The Greeks delighted in wisdom, in playing with ideas, and in the sophistry of "clever mind and cunning tongue."[1] Certainly both the Romans and the Greeks could see Jesus only as a pathetic symbol of weakness.

Yet Jesus came to that ancient world as *power*. That was the word by which Paul described him. Paul was not speaking casually. A Jew by birth, a Roman citizen trained in Greek philosophy, Paul understood the mind and spirit of his times. He knew that his generation cherished wisdom and power, and he could see that Jesus didn't convey that impression. But, Saint Paul said, "to those who are called, both Jews and Greeks, Christ [is] the power of God and the wisdom of God" (1 Corinthians 1:24).

The Greek word for "power," the word Paul used when he described Jesus as "the power of God," is *dunamis*. This is the word, of course, from which we get our word *dynamite*. Here, then, is the power with which God would do his work in the world: the weak power of a baby, the dynamite of God.

Paul knew the power of God in his own life. Before encountering Christ, he had been impregnable in his own sense of righteousness, but Christ—the dynamite of God—had broken through his defenses. There had been a certain smugness in Paul, and a ruthlessness, too: qualities that raise a fortress round a man. But Christ had broken all these barriers—Christ, the dynamite of God. It is such a sensitive power that it could blast through Paul's bitter defenses, yet not leave his life in a shambles. By the same power, Jesus Christ destroyed Paul's lostness and arrogance and built in their place purpose, order, and direction.

What was this power, this weak power, of the Babe born at Christmas? Certainly it is not a matter of organization and leadership. Jesus brought just twelve men together. One of them was a traitor, and nine others were hardly heard from in later years. Only Peter and John made any recorded impact.

I have often heard it said that the secret to Jesus's power was in his teachings, yet this hardly seems an adequate explanation. There have been so many fine teachers through the centuries, but none made a comparable impact on the world. Jesus was a great teacher, but his teachings cannot explain his power.

Others say that the secret of his power was love. Being cursed and rejected, he loved; being crucified, he loved—until, at last, love won, because love lasted longer than hate. But if love was his secret, there must be some further secret, for others have loved but without his power.

Somehow we are forced to confess that there was a power in Jesus that is beyond our explaining; something beyond his teaching, something behind his love. The testimony of the New Testament is that he was the Son of God. Those who knew him firsthand came to such a conclusion, as have millions of others since then. I don't believe there is any other satisfactory explanation for this singular person and his power.

Our generation understands power. We build bombs, transplant organs, and explore space. Yet it becomes increasingly clear that with all our power there is some crucial ineffectiveness in us. We seem somehow to lack the most important power of all. It seems that all our other power will only mean our greater destruction unless we are possessed by the power that can change and redirect us.

Saint Paul called Jesus "the dynamite of God." He observed that when all other power fails, and in areas of life where no other power can reach, the power of Jesus Christ still works.

I'm not sure that our power-conscious generation can understand this, for much power has made us blind to the Greatest Power. But in this season, think deeply when you look at the Bethlehem manger. You will see a helpless, vulnerable baby, an undistinguished carpenter and his wife, and the accompanying signs of human weakness. But remember then what Saint Paul said and what ten millions of others have since found to be true: this baby, Jesus the Christ, is "the wisdom of God" and "the dynamite of God."

Christmas Comes to a University

*C*hristmas comes to all of life. This is the glad word I want to say again and again during this holiday season. Christmas is the story of God coming to earth in Jesus the Christ, and the glory of it is that he came not to one special class, not to a single race, but to all humankind, in all conditions of life. I come now to say with joy that Christmas comes to a university—to academics, scholars, and researchers. That's important news to the whole world, because we live in an age when the work of the scholar affects the style of life of every human being in every corner of our planet. If Christmas did not come to the university, it would miss one of the most strategic and determinative factors of life.

But thanks be to God, the first Christmas came to a university. In fact, the coming of Christmas to the world of the scholar is one of the most familiar and dramatic scenes in the whole Christmas story. Most people don't immediately recognize this fact. We tend to think that progress, learning, and civilization began with us. In many respects, of course, America is only a long generation removed from the frontier, and Western civilization still senses the shadow of the Dark Ages. As a result, we hardly realize what kind of world existed nineteen centuries ago.

But in that first-century world into which Christmas came, a very large percentage of the people were in some measure able to read and write. Some say it was the age of the most widespread literacy our world was to know until some eighteen centuries later. In Palestine, for example, there were schools in every town, with compulsory education for all children over the age of six. Philosophy, law, and rhetoric were in some respects as developed in the first century as they are today. As for medicine, first-century rabbis practiced laws of health that were far ahead of what was done in mid-nineteenth-century Europe and America.

So it was not an illiterate world into which Christmas came. In fact, it was an age when learning was widespread, growing, and generally honored. And in that world, a little group of scholars became part of the Christmas story. We don't know much about them, really. The Bible says simply that they were "wise men from the East" (Matthew 2:1).

We should remember that the lines of study were not so sharply drawn then as they are in our own day. A literate person in the first century was likely to have a good base of available knowledge in a wide variety of fields, rather than being a specialist. We know the wise men were students of astronomy, because they had taken their bearings from a dramatic star. We might also conclude that they were political scientists, because they were coming in search of a new king. They were interpreters of dreams, so we may perhaps say that they were in a measure related to the field of psychiatry.

Weeks, perhaps even months, before that holy night in Bethlehem, a scholar in some Persian center of learning had a flash of insight. Did it come with mathematics, as he calculated the position of the planets? Or with astronomy, as he followed the stars? Or did it come, perhaps, with literature, as he read the writings of the prophets of other generations? However the insight came, a light broke upon him. He gathered together his research team, and they pursued the ray of hope.

What went into their days of planning? Did they discuss their tentative findings in seminars with some of their graduate students before departing? Did they share them with some of their brightest and best? Or was this project so special that they were afraid to mention their findings to any of their professional colleagues? Indeed, did they mention them to some and find themselves laughed out of recognition?

The age in which they lived was shot through with despair. Literature that has come to us from that period shows people living without much hope for the future. One man wrote that the world was perishing and running down and reaching its last end. That's a pretty dismal view, isn't it? But in the first-century world, where many were just so hopeless, there was this little band of scholars who hoped and sought. And at last they came to the end of their journey, a manger in Bethlehem. There they found a peasant couple with a newborn baby. Were they disappointed? One might expect them to be. Surely they were anticipating something more impressive than this! Yet when they found the Babe, they bowed down and worshipped him.

Something about the scene convinced them. They had followed their research to an unlikely end, and now they worshipped.

Is this the missing element in the modern university? George Buttrick once said, "Thought is worthy only when it is marked by reverence."[1] I believe that our knowledge is as badly in need of redemption as is our ignorance. The scholar needs to finish the research at the altar of reverence. Even so, the Christmas scene is made complete when the wise men come to kneel. Christmas comes not only to a back fence, not only to a cave, a hotel, or a church; it also comes to a university.

If the Christmas story did not include the university, it would not have been true to the Bible that records it. The Great Commandment asks that we love God with all our mind, as well as with heart and soul (Matthew 22:37). Surely, then, God's plan of salvation will reach also to the world of the mind. The more alert and trained the mind, the more earnestly one ought to love God with it. The Christmas story needs more than shepherds and angels, innkeeper and worshippers. It must also have a scholar, book and pen in hand, eager to find the truth and to pass it on.

December 14

Christmas Comes to Our Backyard

At its best, this is the time of year when people sing more, laugh more, and love more. At its worst, it is a time when people spend more than they can afford and eat and drink more than they should. It is a time when we reminisce about some of our oldest friends as we read their cards and letters; it is also the time when we find it easiest to strike up new friendships as we wait for service in a department store or travel from one part of the country to another. It is Christmastime, and there is no other day on the calendar that can be compared with it, no other season that makes its mark on the lives of so many people in so many ways. You can love Christmas, as most of us do, or you can dread it, as some surely do; but you can't ignore it.

We, can, however, miss the center, the point and the issue, of the season, which is Jesus Christ. As a matter of fact, in our culture you can very easily miss him. For vast numbers of secular people, Jesus

Christ is just that incidental to the Christmas season; so much so that they think of him, and the religion that bears his name, as an intrusion on their conglomerate of Santa Claus, parties, and shopping.

Our neglect of Jesus is most ironic, of course. And not only because the season bears his name, but also because he is the One we long for even beyond this season. He is what the ancient prophet and several hymn writers call the "desire of nations."

William Sangster reminds us that we human beings have desired God all through the ages. Often we have had admirable pictures of God in our theology and philosophy. Sangster mentions Socrates and Plato, Gautama Buddha, Lao Tzu, and others, as well as the great Hebrew prophets, such as Isaiah and Jeremiah. He reminds us, too, that nature has given us some awesome pictures of God. But all of these remain only pictures, and we human beings needed more.[1]

E. Stanley Jones, the great missionary-evangelist, used to tell the story of a little boy whose father was separated from the family for an extended period. One day, as the boy stood looking at the picture of his father, he turned suddenly to his mother and said, "I wish Father would step out of the picture." That, in the simplest explanation of it, is what the Incarnation and the Christmas story are about: God stepped out of the picture and came among us.

The Bible puts the story in the most specific language. It does not say, "Once upon a time," setting the story in an indefinite, mythical way; it dates the story, as all things were dated in ancient times, by telling us who the rulers were. Matthew tells us that Jesus was born "in the days of Herod the king" (2:1), and Luke adds that it was "when Quirinius was governor of Syria" (2:2), at a time when Caesar Augustus established a special tax. The Bible does not give us a make-believe place or a location with no name; God's unique visit was in Bethlehem, a little inland village that exists to this very day. Indeed, hundreds of thousands of people go there every year, nearly two thousand years later, because of what happened there on the first Christmas.

The human race had long had a picture, sometimes rather distinct, usually clouded, of what God must be like. But at the first Christmas God stepped out of the picture: at a given time, when Herod was ruling Judea and Quirinius was governor of Syria, and at a specific place, a town called Bethlehem.

There is something strategically important about the definite quality of God's appearance at Christmas; not simply from a theological, historical point of view, but because our lives are lived with such specific elements. We need God to meet us, more than twenty centuries later, not in some general, philosophical way but at a given time and a given place, just when and where we especially need such a meeting.

We human beings have hungered for God. There is a divine urge in our hearts that was placed there from the moment of creation. But our impulse toward God is inconsistent and doomed, because with all our stretching and straining we simply cannot touch God. So God, in gracious mercy, bridged the gap that was utterly beyond us. He pursued us, even when we ignored him. He touched us, when we could not possibly reach him. He came to us, when we could not attain him.

We have a good title for God, which we use more often in the Christmas season: Emmanuel. Emmanuel means "God with us." God "became flesh and dwelt among us, full of grace and truth" (John 1:14).

When our daughter Taddy was four years old, a family in our congregation gave a life-sized crèche to the church. The parsonage was next door to the church, and they placed the crèche in the yard right between the parsonage and the church. Taddy awakened from an afternoon nap and looked out on a scene that hadn't been there when she fell asleep. "Look," she exclaimed with a little girl's delight. "They've moved right into our backyard!"

That is, indeed, what God did, and that's what Christmas says. God is not in a faraway place, hurling edicts at us and passing judgments. One day, more than twenty centuries ago, he became flesh and pitched his tent among us. He moved right into our backyard, so that you and I might fully become his sons and daughters.

Christmas Is
for Lonely People

$\mathcal{T}$he Christmas season is the happiest time in all of the year. For some people, at least, that is the case. A great many others, however, will tell you that it is the loneliest and most frustrating of times. Statistics seem to bear them out. There is an increase in suicides during the Christmas season, and psychiatrists report they must deal with many more cases of severe depression. It may be the loveliest time of the year, but for some it is also the loneliest.

It's easy to see why. Christmas is the season of memories. We recall beautiful times from the past; and something peculiar in the human psyche says that the present is not that wonderful, and the future will never quite regain such wonder. We recall as well those times of special pain, and the pain returns with exquisite strength. There is the bereaved person, who thinks back on last Christmas— and many before that—when the circle of love was complete. The pain of bereavement subsides at some points during the year, but it returns in full power at this season.

These feelings are all very real and very valid; but I think the phenomenon of Christmas loneliness goes much deeper. Indeed, it is so much at the heart of our human condition that I am bold to say that Christmas came to deal with the very fact of human loneliness. That is, Christmas is especially for lonely people.

Christmas is often touched by a certain feeling of homesickness. Now that's not surprising, of course. So many of our Christmas delights are related to home. But the homesickness of Christmastime is more than just a human story; it is more than the memories of childhood, more than the poignant recalling of happy days long past. It is the homesickness of the human soul, and it reaches all the way back to the garden of Eden. There is an eternal thing in us, as old as the human race, that knows that we have wandered from home. There are those who try to persuade us otherwise, who say that we are only time-bound creatures conceived in a womb and doomed to end in a tomb; but all of us instinctively know better. Sometimes we wish we were not eternal—we wish we could efface the longing for Eden—but it is impossible to change what we so profoundly are. Every time we have some rush of homesickness—for old friends, for family, for the old neighborhood—it is a homesickness informed by our longing for Eden.

There is another eternal quality of loneliness in Christmas. It is the matter of our unfulfilled dreams. We human beings have certain longings that defy verbalization. Once in a while a poet or a novelist finds words that catch something of the feeling. But most of the time we can find no way to express what we so deeply, ineffaceably feel; this dream of beauty and wholeness that is beyond words and that begins to lose its reality as soon as we try to verbalize it. Where did we get such dreams? How is it that we have longings for something we've never seen or experienced?

Again, this kind of longing is as old as the human race. It is part of our hunger for the divine image we have lost. It reaches back to Eden. And it makes us lonely twice over: first, because in such moments of longing we feel alone within the human race. It's hard to believe that anyone else has such a longing as this. And second, because it makes us feel isolated even from our own psyche. We are possessed by a dream that we ourselves don't understand. There's a kind of ultimate loneliness in that.

Christmas, by its very nature, awakens and makes more painfully sensitive this whole unfulfilled dream. At this season, every year, something in us hopes again. We want to believe that next year will be better, that our best human dreams will be fulfilled. And in that moment of longing, we are made lonely. And here is why: because Christmas is the answer to our eternal homesickness; it is the beginning of the fulfillment of our longings and our impossible dreams.

The basic loneliness of the human heart is the loneliness of displaced persons—of persons, that is, who were meant to live in Eden and who find themselves, instead, at a distance from God. And it is the loneliness of unfulfilled dreams—that is, of persons who were meant to live in the image of God and who struggle instead with failure and frailty; and of persons who were meant to hear the music of heaven but are forced so much of the time to cope with the dissonance of earth.

Christmas comes to heal that basic human loneliness. For Jesus Christ came to our planet to bring us back to God; to bring us back home, that is. Jesus became homeless so that you and I could come home. That's the Christmas story. There was a planet of lonely people who had wandered from home but who could never forget the dream and could never lose their taste for home, no matter how they tried to obliterate it. So he came to this planet to say to all the lonely ones, "You can come home. The Father wants you, and I will show you the way."

No wonder the prophet said, "The people who walked in darkness have seen a great light" (Isaiah 9:2). Does your Christmas season grow shadowed with memories of those loved and lost a while, or thoughts of better days when you enjoyed better health, dearer friends, or more satisfying work? The One who brings light into our darkness can relieve those shadows.

For Christmas comes, especially and profoundly, for lonely people. It invades our loneliness with love and light. If you are lonely this day, or encounter loneliness this season, speak the bright word to your own soul: this is why there was a star and an angel song and a birth in Bethlehem, because God cared about the lonely and sent his Son to find and save them.

December 16

Christmas Is for Workers

Christmastime means laughter and festivities; it means social events and celebrations and pausing before too many tables of cookies and candy and punch. It is such a relaxing, sociable time that we are likely to think Christmas is for those who play. In some ways it is, of course; but from the beginning a quite different matter has also been true: Christmas is for workers.

I think of a Christmas Eve on board a train that was running several hours late. One of the trainmen apologized. "We're running with a short crew tonight. So many of our people call in sick on Christmas Eve." I sympathized with those who yielded to such a temptation, but I was grateful for the railroad men who knew that Christmas was for workers. And I think of those hundreds of thousands of store clerks who have their most trying days of the year in the week before Christmas; and those millions of people who fill every spare moment trying to put together some occasions of taste and beauty for the

Christmas benefit of others. When Christmas Day comes, they sit down in exhaustion. Christmas is for workers.

But of course! After all, the first Christmas came, not to a party in the Bethlehem Hilton, but to a group of workers out on the hillside. "And there were in the same country shepherds abiding in the field, keeping watch over their flock by night" (Luke 2:8 KJV). They were working, and they were the night shift. Have you ever worked a night shift, when all the rest of the world is asleep?

But these shepherds also worked the day shift and the swing shift. That was the nature of their job.

Not only were the shepherds workers, they were among the most despised of workers. We say that all honest work is honorable, but some kinds of work don't bring invitations to the country club. Shepherding was like that in Israel in the first century. Because of the nature of their work, shepherds couldn't keep the ceremonial laws that "good" people kept. Also, their work isolated them from the general company of people, even in many instances from family life, so it was a lonely job. If you were a first-century Jew, you might speak sentimentally about the fact that God had raised a shepherd boy, David, to be Israel's king—but you still didn't want your daughter to marry one.

So the shepherds were out in the fields working that Christmas night. These were rugged men. Their hands were dirty from their work, their faces lined from living outdoors, and their bodies smelled of animals, dust, and perspiration. They were workers: men such as you might find on a loading dock, at the lunch counter of a truck stop, in the foundry, or cleaning manure from a barn. And Christmas came to them right where they were—at work.

Don't be surprised that Christmas came to people while they were on the job. I can't think of an instance when God called someone who was loafing. Moses saw the burning bush when he was out on a hillside herding sheep. Samuel had to call young David in from the fields in order to crown him king, and Nehemiah was working as a servant in a king's palace when he was called by God to go back to Jerusalem and help rebuild the city. So, some workers hurried into the birthplace of the Messiah that first Christmas night.

Thirty years later Jesus gave special glory to work. "My Father is always working," he said, "and I too must work" (John 5:17 GNT). What kind of work did Jesus do? As you follow him through the days of his ministry, you see him teaching the multitudes, healing the sick, blessing children, casting out demons, and listening to and talking with those who were generally scorned by society. The Bible says, on repeated occasions, that he was "moved with compassion" as he saw the needs of those around him. In all of this he fulfilled the prophecy of Isaiah: "Surely He hath borne our griefs, and carried our sorrows" (Isaiah 53:4a KJV).

At first thought, the fact that the first Christmas came to workers seems very remarkable because our idea of Christmas is all celebration and fun. But further thought says that it is just right. Of course Christmas would come to workers! Christmas means that God himself came to our planet in Jesus Christ because there was work to be done. All its inhabitants were heavy-laden, some with the heartbreak of life, some with counterfeit pleasures, and some with the sheer burden of living. So he came to enter into the perspiration of life, to pull and strain at humanity's heavy load.

And since Jesus came to do the hardest of all work—carrying humanity's grief, sorrow, and sin—how better can we celebrate Christmas than to become workers? If you want to be sure of Christmas this year, enter into the spirit of the One who came to our world to work at human burdens and who calls us to do the same. Seek today and tomorrow and every day for the burdened, the lonely, the forgotten, the heavy-laden. Take some burden you could so easily escape, some problem that is not at all yours. Relieve someone's pain by drawing a little of it into yourself. Place food on some table, mercy in some life. And as you do, in simple human love and Christian faith, Christmas will come upon you all unbidden. It may be as bright as an angel song or as unpretentious as a sleeping flock, but it will come, because Christmas is for workers. God is working in his world, and we must work, too.

December 17

Christmas Is
for Spendthrifts

A few days ago we turned to the magi as role models for us. In this season when we do so much gift-giving, they are exemplary as three wise shoppers. Unless you look at the price tag, that is.

A season of gift-giving means a season of shopping. And a season of shopping means a season of spending. Retailers count on it being so. They rely on this time of year for a disproportionate percentage of their year's bottom line.

Sometimes all the spending gives us pause. We may worry that we are spending too much individually. And beyond our individual patterns we wonder if we as a society spend too much money at this time of year. It may be good for the economy, but it does not seem good for the soul. It smacks of materialism and commercialization.

There's no doubt that Christmas has become very commercial. That reflects our human nature, in both its glory and its greed. Our minds see the potential in nearly every circumstance (that's good), and then we easily get carried away with an insatiable appetite for more (and that's bad).

Yet I wonder—if the magi lived in our day, or if we had lived in theirs—I wonder if we would think that they were too materialistic. I wonder if we would criticize them for spending too much. For they surely did spend!

You remember how it unfolded. At the time of Jesus's birth, some scholars in the eastern world had concluded, partly from their study of the planets and no doubt partly from divine insight, that a new King of the Jews was to be born. These wise men found their way to Bethlehem and bowed in worship before the baby Jesus, and in their adoration they presented gifts to him: gold, frankincense, and myrrh. It is in the gifts of these wise men that the human side of the tradition of Christmas giving was first established.

When we decry the materialism of Christmas giving, we should remember that these first Christmas gifts were highly materialistic: they were items from the first-century equivalent of an exclusive shop. When we complain about the rat race of Christmas shopping, I ponder the wise men: Did they do a frantic shopping routine before they set out on their journey? Did they ask themselves, their wives, and their respected counselors, "What do you think we should buy for a new king?"

And have you imagined what it was like when they returned home? They try to tell their wives or some of their scholarly colleagues about their experience. They recall the remarkable way the star guided them, their conversation with the scribes in Jerusalem, and the unexpected climax to their journey at an exceedingly humble setting in Bethlehem. And how they pushed straw and manure aside to lay down their expensive gifts.

Now I hear someone interrupting the wise men. "You say the mother is a peasant girl and the man with her a village carpenter? And they were in some scroungy, back-of-the-barn place? And you gave the baby gold, frankincense, and myrrh? You gave this poor little Jewish kid all those expensive things? What in the world made you do that?" And I hear the men answering lamely, "It just seemed the right thing to do." Christmas, you see, is for spendthrifts—for those who spend extravagantly and recklessly. The giving it inspires defies logic.

Isn't that the philosophy of our gift wrapping? Mind you, I'm a paper saver; my family members shake their heads in despair on Christmas morning as I carefully collect the smooth portions of all those expensive papers so I can reuse them on smaller presents next Christmas. But I'm glad for the glamorous wrappings, illogical as they are. That's the principle, too, of such very practical gifts as fruit baskets and cheese delicacies. The fruit doesn't come in a plastic bag, nor the cheese in cling wrap, but with frills and color and bows and design. "Phony," someone might say. "Like frankincense and myrrh," I would reply. And so, too, it is with our homemade products of the season. The cookies are cut and designed; the candies are some you only make once a year; the settings for Christmas dinner are somehow special. Christmas not only means giving, it means giving with a flourish.

And the issue of it all is this: that the special quality of Christmas giving is love. Christmas giving that is done purely for business reasons, with no real affection or regard for the recipient, violates the Christmas spirit. So, too, does giving that tries to keep up with the other person or that tries to impress others. But the fact that some pervert and abuse Christmas giving is no reason for abandoning it. To the contrary, we should redeem it. Let us return to the spirit of the first Christmas, when wise men shopped carefully to find just the right things for a new king, then brought their peculiarly inappropriate gifts to a poor baby in Bethlehem.

But let us go back further than that. The tradition of Christmas giving is older and more profound than the wise men. The Gospel of John tells us where Christmas giving began, in words so familiar that we forget they describe the Christmas spirit: "For God so loved the world, that he gave his only begotten Son, that whosoever believeth in him should not perish, but have everlasting life" (John 3:16 KJV). Christmas giving began with God.

Have no doubt about it: God was a spendthrift. There was an irrational abandon in his giving. Logic would say there must have been an easier way to reach the human soul, a gift less dramatic and less costly. But God gave his Son. When God gave his only begotten Son, he was a spendthrift. He was absurdly, irrationally generous. There is no logic that can justify such a gift.

So I'm sorry that Christmas giving has gotten a bad name in recent years. The giving we do is all to the good, if it comes from love. True, some pervert the giving, some exploit, and some do it thoughtlessly. But the giving is good. It brings out the best in us, when we let it. And it is of the very heart of Christmas. The wise men gave us the human example with their fanciful, almost absurd gifts for a little peasant baby. But far more significant, God set the pattern. God, caring not how undeserving the recipients were, gave the only really priceless One in the universe, and gave in love. God was a spendthrift, and Christmas, still, is for all loving spendthrifts. Give, and be glad.

Christmas Is for Saints

Somehow the saints' part in the Christmas story has never really caught the public fancy; not, at least, since the biblical writers. The New Testament gives a bit more space to the story of two saints at Christmastime—Simeon and Anna—than it does to either the shepherds or the wise men. But since then, not many have noticed them.

Let me tell you about these saints. Simeon was apparently an elderly man, and the Bible tells us that he was a good and pious man. Anna was also elderly. She had been a widow for many years, and she came to the temple day after day, year after year, "worshiping with fasting and prayer night and day" (Luke 2:37).

The law of their faith required that Jewish parents should have their boy babies circumcised at a given time, then come with the new baby to the temple for an act of purification. Joseph and Mary made their appointed pilgrimage, expecting, I'm sure, that it would be a very quiet affair. No one in Jerusalem knew them. They were an unpretentious peasant couple; there was no compelling reason to give them attention.

Yet attention came. First, it was Simeon, awesome not only for his age and bearing but because he was so profoundly moved by the sight of the little family. He took the baby in his arms and began to thank God.

> Lord, now lettest thou thy servant depart in peace,
> according to thy word;
> for mine eyes have seen thy salvation
> which thou hast prepared in the presence of all peoples,
> a light for revelation to the Gentiles,
> and for glory to thy people Israel. (vv. 29-32)

Joseph and Mary marveled at what was happening.

Then Anna came to them. She was a prophetess, the Bible tells us; and when she saw the baby, she also gave thanks to God, then "spoke of him to all who were looking for the redemption of Jerusalem" (v. 38). She spread the good news wherever she could.

Most of us ought to feel closer to Simeon and Anna than to the shepherds and the wise men. There is a sense that the participants in the Christmas story are symbolic of the various kinds of conversion to Christianity. The shepherds are like the dramatic conversions: people saved from alcoholism and gambling, or like Saul of Tarsus, struck by a dramatic revelation. The wise men are like those people who follow an intellectual search: perhaps for years they look at the evidence and the problems, for a while almost lose their way, then experience that special kind of intuition that leads them at last to the reality of Jesus

Christ. Simeon and Anna are like that great body of persons who live earnest, generally good lives, until one day they are led to the fullness of Jesus Christ.

To my mind, the most impressive matter in the story of Simeon and Anna is this: they waited. Does that sound altogether uninspiring? Frankly, it is; but it strikes me that saints do a lot of waiting. Others grow impatient with causes and with people, but saints keep on waiting.

Some years ago a writer analyzed what was happening in the slums of Boston. It was during a time of renewed social consciousness, especially on the part of the young. The writer said that residents in the area had gotten a bit cynical about it all. Bright young men and women came into the neighborhood each year full of enthusiasm and promises of social revolution. And a few months later they were gone, and a new crew was coming in. They had plenty of enthusiasm and exciting ideas but no staying power. By contrast, the writer noted some priests, nuns, and mission workers—both black and white, Catholic and Protestant—went on working in the area year after year. They were without fanfare or glamor, but they stayed. Saints do a lot of waiting.

The same thing can surely be said about our dealings with individuals. Almost all of us are humane enough to give a pat on the back, to speak a helpful word, or to encourage a student after a failure or two. But the saints are those who keep on believing and waiting.

Obviously, waiting is not idleness. Indeed, it is very hard work. Not only do routine tasks themselves become tedious, but it is so difficult to keep faith. When we read that Anna came to the temple day and night at eighty-four years of age, that she fasted and prayed, we see a stalwart example of a saint who was waiting. Lesser souls rise with enthusiasm and fall off as time goes by, but the great souls keep on waiting, believing, expecting. Simeon, Luke tells us, had been "waiting for the consolation of Israel" (Luke 2:25 KJV); and because he waited so earnestly, God revealed that he would not die until he had seen the Messiah. Did he sometimes say to God, "Have you forgotten? Have you noticed, perhaps, that I'm getting older?" But he kept on waiting, because saints are very good at waiting.

Saints wait because they are fed by hope. Animal enthusiasm wanes as quickly as it rises, but hope has inner resources by which it is renewed. When the wind blows fiercely or the road grows steep, others lose heart. But the saints remain steady.

At this season, hope comes anew to all; and with hope we rise up to meet the disheartening and the impossible. But the saints carry this spirit with them all through the year. They keep watching, waiting, and hoping. They believe in God and in his Christ; and because of their belief, they will not give up. Because they wait, Christmas comes to them. Not so dramatically, perhaps, as to the shepherds or the wise men. But it comes, and it stays. Indeed, the coming they experience may be the best of all.

December 19

The Man Who Tried
to Steal Christmas

*I*n 1957 Dr. Seuss wrote *How the Grinch Stole Christmas*. More than twenty centuries earlier, there was a king who tried to steal Christmas. His name was Herod.

In many ways he was a good king. He was a great builder; the temple in Jerusalem was evidence of that. Sometimes he was generous. In hard times he remitted taxes to make things easier for the people. During the famine of 25 BC, he melted down his own gold plate to buy corn for the hungry.

But Herod was extremely—indeed, insanely—fearful of his position. He murdered his wife and her mother and, eventually, three of his sons, because he was afraid they might try to take his throne. Emperor Augustus commented bitterly that it was safer to be Herod's pig than Herod's son. When Herod was seventy years old and felt he would soon die, he ordered the imprisonment of the most distinguished citizens of Jerusalem and commanded that the moment he died, they should all be killed. He knew no one would mourn his death, but he was determined some tears should be shed when he died.

This is the man who was on the throne the star-bright night when Jesus was born. Imagine, then, his feeling when wise men from a far country suddenly appeared in his royal court, reporting that their studies revealed that a king was to be born in that area and asking in the king's palace for further information.

In Dr. Seuss's Christmas story, the Grinch dressed in a Santa Claus suit in order to carry out his effort to steal Christmas. Herod did something similar. He said to the wise men, "When you find this newborn king, come back and tell me where he is, so that I may go and worship him too." But the wise men were warned by God of Herod's true intentions, so they returned home by another way.

Frustrated and angry, Herod resolved to get the potential king at any cost. Someone who will kill members of his own family to protect his throne is not likely to be distressed at the death of unknown infants. Herod sent his soldiers into Bethlehem with instructions to kill every child under two years of age. A few lives didn't matter to him; they were a small price to protect his throne.

It's a brutal story, yet there is a sense in which Herod's understanding of Christmas was better than that which most people entertain. He realized that someday the baby would grow up.

So many people—good people, nothing like Herod—find Christmas far more to their liking than Easter or Good Friday. They haven't stopped to analyze it, but it is altogether possible that they have something of the same problem as Herod. They don't really want the baby to grow up. Of course they would never be party to Herod's brutality. But they would manage, if possible, to keep the baby from becoming King.

Here, you see, is the challenge of the Christian faith. Jesus was born to be King. We are inclined to limit him to a world of sentiment, of comfort, of understanding sympathy; and believe me, he is all these things. But he must also be King. It is an easier thing to sing, "Away in a Manger" than to sing, "Lead On, O King Eternal." It is more pleasant to think of Jesus snuggled in a bed of hay where the cattle are lowing than to hear him say, "If anyone would follow Me, he must take up his cross daily."

Herod was terrified that perhaps the baby born in Bethlehem would someday be King. We, too, are afraid he might want to become King—that perhaps he will want a larger share of our money, or he will frown on the way we treat some people or talk about them, or he will call us to do some unpleasant task. But we are more sophisticated than Herod. We accept Christmas, even glory in it; but we make Jesus a prisoner of Christmas.

Herod was frightened about this unknown baby in Bethlehem because he thought he might take from him the throne of Judea. No. Jesus would have let Herod remain king of Judea, but he would have asked Herod to cease being king of Herod.

So Jesus says to us, "I'll let you go on managing your business, your profession, and your home, but I want to manage you. You can be president of the club, captain of the team, or manager of the firm. But I want to be King of your life." Herod had no idea what kind of king Jesus was meant to be.

Dr. Seuss's story of the Grinch ends happily. The Grinch has a change of heart; and instead of stealing Christmas, he discovers it and makes it his own. But Herod's story does not end happily.

Wouldn't it have been wonderful if Herod's small heart had been touched? Can you imagine him coming, in splendor and pomp, to that cave in back of the hotel and kneeling in the cow dung so he can lay his crown at the foot of the manger? If he had, Herod would have died a beloved and happy man. He would have become a great king of Judea, if only he had let Jesus become King of Herod.

The same promise comes to us. If we will let the Babe of Bethlehem become our King, Christmas will come true. The sentiment will still be there, but with a foundation of reality. There will still be singing, but now your voice will become part of the angel chorus. There will still be a light in the sky, but now the light will shine in, and from, your own heart.

Jesus was born not to forever be a baby but to become King. And the throne he desires most of all is the throne of your heart.

The Divine View

So many pictures come to mind with the word *Christmas*. We think of decorated trees, music in the stores, bell-ringing Santas, parties, Christmas cards, and seeing still another showing of our favorite holiday movies. We think of a Christmas pageant and a choir concert, getting home to be with family or bringing the family home, meeting trains and planes and watching weather reports, and opening packages on Christmas Eve or Christmas Day, according to our family's tradition.

These are all lovely pictures, and I savor their flavor as much as anyone. There's only one thing wrong with these pictures: they center too exclusively on the human side of Christmas. For Christmas, you see, is first and above all else a religious event. It is God's story before it is ours.

Christmas began with God. He came into our world in a unique, once-and-for-all way, to dwell among us. And he did so, the Scriptures tell us, so that anyone who will receive him might have the power to become sons and daughters of God.

Now, let us observe at the outset that this story is hard to believe. From a cold, rational point of view, it is hard to imagine God, Creator of the universe, being so concerned about one species of inhabitants (out of almost innumerable species) on one speck of a planet (out of millions of heavenly bodies) that he would make a kind of cloak-and-dagger visit to this particular planet.

And, of course, the story becomes still more difficult to believe as it unfolds. He not only comes to this planet, he comes as a helpless creature. He enters the world with a measure of mystery, via an extraordinary conception, yet he is born through the process of groans and bursting water and blood. An umbilical cord must be cut, then tied; and before long the newborn must be clasped to a breast and nourished, else he will die. And in this particular instance, the baby draws his first earthly breath in the heavy air of a stable, in the midst of flies and animal sounds and crawling things. See this little creature of ruddy face and hungry mouth, and ask yourself if you really believe the Christmas story as the Bible tells it.

As Madeleine L'Engle ponders the wonder of such a story as this, she confesses that "it's not the secular world which presents me with problems about Christmas, it's God."[1] Our secular celebration is sometimes both painful and absurd in its misuse of this season, but we can understand these human frailties because we're so accustomed to them. God's peculiarities, however, are something else again! How do we comprehend such love, such pursuit of the human creature, such divine condescension?

We have a word for this: *incarnation*. It is related to the word *carnal*, which means "fleshly." Incarnation means for something to come in the flesh. So the Bible tells us that "the Word became flesh and dwelt among us" (John 1:14).

Yet, even when the Word becomes flesh, there is a problem of communication. No matter how distinctly you may speak, there is the question of my hearing. When someone speaks English, I can distinguish the words; but when someone speaks a language entirely unknown to me, I hear nothing but an amalgam of sounds—a potpourri of grunts and sibilants and accents. So, too, when God's Christ comes to our lives, some of us do not hear him well. We are so accustomed to speaking hate and fear and arrogance that we find it hard to understand his language of love and peace and humility. It is the mercy and goodness of God that he would subject Himself to our poor hearing, and even poorer perceiving, in order that he might communicate with us.

So it is that our images of Christmas are distorted. It is, indeed, the season of giving, so he has given his only begotten Son; but we reject his gift. It is a season for celebrating, so he has sent out invitations to the grandest of parties; but we sometimes do not even grant him the courtesy of a reply. It is the season of loving, so he has loved us with his very blood; but we have gone blithely on our way, not even acknowledging his love.

I wonder how God feels at Christmastime? We hurry through the season he gave us, missing the point of it and wondering why it isn't better. For its name, the holiday takes the title by which his Son is known—Christ-mas; and for multitudes, that is the last recognition that he has anything to do with it. Yet the holiday is his, and he gave it to us.

Before this season is past I will so often write and say, "Merry Christmas!" It is a grand phrase, and we cannot use it too much. But this year I would like, in the simplicity and directness of a child, to turn the phrase back to the One who made it possible. I would like to say, "Merry Christmas, God, I hope you haven't been too disappointed in the presents we've given you or the casualness with which we've treated your invitations. I'd like for this day, in my heart, to be everything you want it to be. Merry Christmas, dear God!"

December 21

I Believe in Joy

The Christmas season has a special vocabulary. It's not that we add new words to our daily speech but that we give a larger place to some old words that are otherwise often on the back shelf . . . words like *peace*, *joy*, and *love*, for instance.

So let me celebrate Christmas by affirming that I believe in joy. I don't mean to put this statement on a level with "I believe in God, the Father Almighty, maker of heaven and earth." But because I am convinced of the truths enunciated in the Apostles' and the Nicene Creeds, I have a basis for the workaday creed, which finds expression in a line like "I believe in joy." The joy of which I speak cannot exist except that God so loved the world that he visited us in Jesus Christ.

Joy was a dominant theme the first Christmas night: "I bring you good news of a great joy which will come to all the people" (Luke 2:10). That was the angelic message to the shepherds that night.

Joy. You can't speak of Christmas with a Christian accent and leave out that word. Secular society can speak of parties, fun, and feasting; it can even speak of giving and of peace. But the Christian word inseparably linked with Christmas is *joy*. God broke upon our world with love, thrusting salvation full in our paths!

If God cares enough about us human creatures, individually, that he would send his Son to redeem us, and if our lives can be made whole and meaningful and victorious as a result of that action—if all of that be true, as I believe it is—then Christmas does indeed mean joy.

Jesus brought the word to life during his earthly ministry. As he healed the sick and brought peace to confused minds, the people went from him with a leap and a laugh. Jesus was a man of joy, so full of life and laughter that little children flocked to him and adults wanted him to come to their dinner parties. Wherever he went, he brought life and joy. "'I came that [you] may have life,'" Jesus said, "'and have it abundantly'" (John 10:10b).

This joy that Jesus had and that he gave to others was never artificial nor superficial; it was at the very core of life. Since this was so, the transient circumstances of life had little effect on his joy. On the night before his crucifixion, Jesus explained to his disciples that persecution lay ahead for them, and a cross for him. Yet he said that he wanted his joy to be in them and for their joy to be complete (John 15:11). He warned that they would soon pass through a period of mourning, but he promised their grief would turn to joy, and it was a joy no one could take from them (John 16:22).

But I'm sorry to say that the Christian church hasn't always seemed to believe in joy. Many people's religion seems to be a painful thing for them. To tell you the truth, I'm not even sure Christianity is solemn, let alone painful. It is serious, and it deals with the most serious issues of human life. But painful—never! If Christianity is true to its Founder, it is a religion of joy.

Paul Tillich said that it is "reality that gives joy, and reality alone." He notes that the Bible speaks so often of joy because the Bible "is the most realistic of all books."[1] Ignoring reality can give fun, but it can never give joy. Perhaps one of our most pathetic errors is that we try to substitute fun for joy and often mistake the two. Fun is largely an external thing, superimposed from the outside, while joy springs up from within. Fun is almost completely dependent upon circumstances, while joy has next to nothing to do with circumstances. Fun can sometimes have a malicious or an immoral quality, while joy is pure. Joy, as we noted, can never be superficial or artificial; joy is at the very core of being, and it cannot be had without reality.

But if joy cannot be put on from the outside, where does a person find it? Tillich says that people of the Bible felt that "the lack of joy is a consequence of man's separation from God, and the presence of joy is a consequence of the reunion with God."[2] So joy comes when we are linked with God, the Source of life.

Joy is such a key word in the vocabulary of Christmas. Christmas says that God so loved our world that he gave his only begotten Son to reunite this world with himself. There is no wonder, then, that the angel told the shepherds, "I bring you good news of a great joy," and no wonder the angel promised that this joy would be "to all the people." If joy depended upon economics or culture or talent, all could not lay claim to it; but since it comes from union with God, and God has already extended himself to make that union possible, it is here for us all.

So I believe in joy. I expect it. It is part of my birthright in Jesus Christ, and when I live without it, it is because I have allowed someone or something—most likely myself!—to interfere with what God had in mind. Joy came as part of Jesus's birth announcement. Heaven forbid that we should live as if Jesus had never been born!

The Dark Joy

*A*s we explored yesterday, *joy* is the word for Christmas. If any single word can characterize the mood and emotion of the season, it must certainly be joy.

We see how many of the carols take joy as their theme. And beyond the songs that declare the point in precise and obvious phrases, joy is the mood of all the carols, even when the word is not used. Most of us sing Christmas music in a rollicking style, which we rarely use for the rest of church music—more's the pity. But the music is after the fact. That is, the music didn't make the joy, the joy made the music.

Yet in the midst of all that joy, playing like a countertheme, there's another mood—a subtle shadow over Christmas. In the midst of the gaiety, there is a sense of unease. For the heritage of the first Christmas is the heritage of a shadowed kind of joy. Let me call it a dark joy.

Saint Luke tells us of a frightening word that was spoken to Mary. It came from the old man, Simeon, who gave thanks to God when he saw the baby and recognized him to be the awaited Messiah. Simeon declared a prophetic blessing on the baby; but in the midst of the blessing he spoke this warning to the mother: "And a sword will pierce through your own soul also" (Luke 2:35a).

What a strange thing to say to a new mother, especially while telling her that her son was to be a light for the Gentiles, the glory of Israel, and the salvation of all people. "And a sword will pierce through your own soul." In the midst of the joy, this sharp pain thrust into the heart of the promise, this mystical threat. It's hard to imagine that Mary understood at that moment what Simeon was saying. Perhaps the old man's words came back to her many times during Jesus's growing-up years, and she wondered, "Is this what he meant?" And the pain became more intense—the sword more piercing—as Jesus began his public ministry and met with so much opposition and ridicule. And then, of course, came the cross.

Simeon's words anticipated the pain that lay ahead. Yet his words are not the only foreshadowing of the cross and the tomb contained within the Christmas story. We think, too, of the gifts of the magi.

A church Christmas pageant is hardly complete without the stately entrance of the wise men, singing words by John H. Hopkins, "We Three Kings of Orient Are." You recall that the first and last verses have the three wise men singing together. But the second, third, and fourth verses call for individual kings to sing of their particular gifts—gold, frankincense, and myrrh. Have you pondered the strange message the third wise man sings?

> Myrrh is mine; its bitter perfume
> breathes a life of gathering gloom;
> sorrowing, sighing, bleeding, dying,
> sealed in the stone-cold tomb.[1]

What strange words for a Christmas song! What was Hopkins trying to say? He was playing on the significance in the gift of myrrh. This fragrant resin was used not only as a perfume or an anointing oil but, as mentioned earlier, also in the ancient burial process. Thus when Jesus was buried, Nicodemus brought a mixture of myrrh and aloes to be placed with his body.

But the story does not end at Calvary, nor in the myrrh, which anoints for burial. The poet concludes the story rightly in his account of the three wise men:

> Glorious now behold Him arise;
> King and God and sacrifice:
> Alleluia, Alleluia,
> sounds through the earth and skies.

Notice the Christmas pattern: joy—darkness—then far greater joy. The joy of the first Christmas had a dark shadow so that there might be a greater joy. This is why Jesus came; not for the brief beauty of Bethlehem, but for the eternal triumph of Calvary.

If the manger had not led to the cross—if the journey of his life had led simply from manger to high and worthy achievement as great teacher, notable leader—there would have been no more reason for rejoicing at Bethlehem's manger than at any one of hundreds of other birthplaces. The angels sang, not because he was born, but because he was born to die. The real joy of Christmas is inextricably bound up with its sorrow. If there were no sorrow at the manger, no sword piercing the heart of Mary, there would be no eternal reason to sing.

So perhaps much of our Christmas celebrating actually sells Christmas short. Perhaps much of our celebrating is superficial, one-dimensional, never coming to the point. We do well, of course, to enjoy the spirit of goodwill, the cards and presents and parties. And it is lovely to enjoy those warm sentiments that so characterize this season, even for the least religious: the feeling of kindness toward our fellow creatures and our general sense of gratitude. All of these responses are fine and beautiful; so fine and beautiful, in fact, that there's a danger we may stop there. And if we do, we will miss the heart of it all.

For Christmas, you see, is the story of salvation. Please, then, let us not settle for a story of sentiment, no matter how lovely it may be, for it is so far short of the total story. Christmas is the season of love; but let us remember that the source of that love is in God, not just a loveliness of the moment. Christmas is the season of giving. But it begins with God's great gift of himself through Jesus Christ, the Gift we need most.

There is, indeed, joy in Christmas. I have called it a dark joy, but my word is not the best one. What Christmas offers is not really a dark joy but a deep joy. It is a joy beyond the moment, beyond the light laughter, beyond the passing touch. It is the joy of eternity, the profound laughter of the ages, the full embrace of God. Take joy, the deep joy of Christmas.

The Dark Road to Bethlehem

*T*he most memorable Advent season of my life came sometime in my midteens; I think it was the winter of 1938. It was like every other Christmas in those years of my life. Nearly every evening was spent at church, practicing the annual Christmas pageant, then a two- or three-block walk home through the snow.

It happened that on all of those evenings, the Iowa skies were gloriously clear. One night, looking up into the mass of stars, I began singing about that long-ago "midnight clear" when angels were "bending near the earth, to touch their harps of gold"; and as I sang, I was carried in my teenage imagination to some Judean hillside I had never seen. Every evening after that, through the rest of Advent and into Christmastide, I was able to evoke the same feeling of gladness and beauty. That's why I will never forget that Advent season, when the starlit skies made so real to me a midnight clear, centuries before. It seemed, on those evenings, that I was part of the shepherd story.

Many years passed before I realized that the "midnight clear" was only in poet Edmund Sears's imagination. The Bible doesn't tell us what kind of night it was, whether cloudy or clear, starlit or pitch dark. We know that when the angels appeared to the shepherds, "the glory of the Lord shone round about them" (Luke 2:9 KJV), but we don't know what the sky was like during the hours preceding that angelic visitation. Nor do we know whether the shepherds ran to Bethlehem in a path of brightness, or whether they had to pick their way through midnight darkness.

But while we don't know anything specific about the sky or the weather conditions the night Jesus was born, we do know something about the kind of world into which he was born, and this I can tell you: it was dark.

Take the world of first-century politics, for example. Mind you, it was a world of peace, but it was peace that was maintained by the powerful threat of the Roman army. Socially, it was even darker. Human life was cheap, because the very structure of the Roman Empire was built on slavery. Throughout much of the world there was little mercy for blind persons, those who were poor, persons with disabilities, or those who were very old. It was a world that hardly knew the meaning of compassion.

But that's the whole point of the Christmas story. Jesus came to the world not because it was bright and happy, gracious and good but because it was a world in need. God was compelled by our human need. God so loved the world, not because it was attractive and winsome, but because it so needed divine love. Call him the Savior, and you acknowledge that it was a world lost in sin; call him the Prince of Peace, and you confess that it was a world consumed by war; call him the Light of the World, and you recognize that he came into a place of darkness.

It was a dark road to Bethlehem. I find that marvelously reassuring. I rejoice that Jesus came into the dark place of human need. Christmas—the season of carols and parties, of celebration and laughter—came into existence because the world was in a dark season.

And he comes still, for all our dark seasons. What happened so long ago is not limited to that single event nor even to our continuing annual celebrations. Whenever and however a dark season comes, it is a signal of the potential for the divine light; for Jesus came to make our midnights clear.

It matters not what the darkness may be, the light is magnificently effective. Whether the dark world of totalitarian oppression or the subtle darkness of personal arrogance, whether the time of economic depression or the depression of inexplicable loneliness, always his light can break through our darkness.

So I think I understand why Edmund Sears wrote as he did. Whatever the physical nature of that night when Jesus was born, Sears felt the "clearness" of it. And, of course, I sang this hymn with such exuberant conviction during that long-ago, teenage Advent season for the same reason. My clothing was modest; the home to which I was walking was, I now realize, little more than a shanty. I was beset by the uncertainties that pursue nearly all teenagers, including, as I recall, unrequited love. As I think back on it, it was really a rather dark road, with poverty and its own kind of adolescent loneliness.

But it was midnight clear! The dark road was lighted by the strong glory of Jesus Christ, who had come into the world to save the lost and dispel the darkness. That's why I sang each evening as I walked through the snow. And that's why I still recommend the Lord of Bethlehem and Calvary. If at this moment your road is dark, hear this: whatever the darkness, there is light in Jesus Christ. Your darkness can not shut him out; indeed, it is because of the darkness that he came. For you—he came for you.

December 24

The Night of the Great Spectacular

*C*hristmas is a festival of lights.

Our modern celebration of Christmas is a grand demonstration of electrical power. We turn on lights—literally millions of them. Nearly every home, including even very poor homes, will have anything from a handful to a hundred lights on its Christmas tree, and a scattering of lights elsewhere in the house and yard. Downtown and each neighborhood shopping area are set alive with hundreds of small bulbs.

But the spectacular quality of Christmas did not begin with the discovery of the electric light bulb. That mood was present in the celebration through long centuries when light was hard to come by. As Martin Luther was walking home one Christmas Eve more than four hundred years ago, he was awestruck by the thousands of stars in the clear winter sky, and by the beauty of the majestic evergreens.

It seemed that the stars were literally clinging to the branches of the trees. When he reached home, Luther tried to explain the glory of the scene to his wife and children, but he could find no adequate words. So he cut down a small fir and placed lighted candles on it to represent the starry sky above the stable on the night that Christ was born.

For more than three hundred years afterwards, until the invention of the light bulb, our ancestors placed candles on their Christmas trees to bring light to their celebration. But there were hundreds of other ways that light was part of ancient and medieval celebrations. In some European lands it was customary to place candles in windows to guide the Christ Child to shelter. The Irish placed a candle in the window then left the door open to attract the Holy Family. In Serbia, in other days, the head of the family would light a candle on Christmas Eve and pray that the crops would be abundant in the new year. And in Bulgaria, peasants would go to the stables with lighted tapers and say to the animals, "The Child is born and blesses you tonight."

It's not surprising that we use light for our Christmas celebration, for Christmas began with a blaze of light. We think so often of the first Christmas as a nighttime setting: Joseph and Mary seeking lodging for the night, the shepherds watching their flocks by night, the wise men following a nighttime star. But we forget that into that night came a blaze of light. The first Christmas was the night of the Great Spectacular.

You know all about spectaculars, of course. We live in the age of the spectacular. Our age has Hollywood and neon signs and Madison Avenue and television and iPads and fluorescent lights. But—let me say it reverently—our age has nothing to compare with the night of the Great Spectacular, which occurred two millennia ago. A baby was to be born in a village in Palestine, and it was important that the birth should be recognized and recorded as an event. So the whole universe came to assist in making a Spectacular. Far in the East a star burst forth in particular glory and moved through the sky for weeks until it suspended in majestic expectancy over the place where the young Child lay. In another place, an angel appeared to a group of shepherds; and when the angel had made an announcement of the baby's birth, he was surrounded by a multitude—hundreds, thousands, who can say?—of other angels, and the whole magnificent chorus broke into a paean of praise such as the world had never heard.

Hundreds of years before, the prophet Isaiah had imagined and envisioned such an occasion, and he had spoken of it in the language of light: "The people who walked in darkness," he said—and certainly it was such a world, a world living in darkness—

> The people who walked in darkness
>> have seen a great light;
> those who dwelt in a land of deep darkness,
>> on them has light shined. (Isaiah 9:2)

Here was the fact the first Christians faced: their lives had so often been lives of darkness, and their meeting with Jesus had been a meeting with light. They knew from experience what it was to walk in the land of the "shadow of death," and then have the light shine upon them (Matthew 4:16). Take Matthew, for instance. When he writes in his Gospel about the birth of Jesus, and about the wise men seeing the star and following it, he is not only telling the facts of Jesus's birth as they have been reported to him; he is also telling the facts of Jesus's birth as he has himself experienced Christ. Matthew remembers when he was a tax collector, lost and alienated from God and in darkness; and one day Jesus walked by his tax booth, and light flooded his life. So, when Matthew writes that the wise men followed a star with exceeding great joy, you can almost hear him whisper, "And I have followed too!"

That's the way I read the Christmas story—and you may, too. I think of a time when I was in darkness . . . and when darkness was in me. But Jesus Christ broke into my darkness, bringing me light. So, then, when I read the story of the night of the Great Spectacular, the night of Jesus's birth, with its star and angel chorus and blinding light, my heart says, "It's true, it's true! For the light has shone upon me."

That's why some of us turn on special lights at Christmastime. We have to because of the light that has come into our lives. And how about you? What do the Christmas lights mean to you? If they mean less than this, perhaps you've missed something, because Christmas is not only a spectacular night long ago. It is a life of light today.

Christmas Word: Salvation

*W*hen I was a boy there was a Methodist church in my hometown that was located right in the midst of taverns, secondhand stores, pawn shops, and cheap hotels. It had a sign out front in the shape of a cross. The horizontal bar read "God Is Love." Intersecting, the vertical bar declared "Jesus Saves."

In some settings the church sign might have seemed garish, but there on lower Fourth Street it had a redeeming dignity. It was surrounded by such motley appeals: "Secondhand Suits," "Rooms for Men," "Jewelry Bought and Sold" and then, magnificently, "God Is Love: Jesus Saves."

If any five words, or any two lines, could tell the Christmas story, these are the ones. And if any setting is appropriate to the spirit of Christmas, this is it. For while Christmas now conjures, in most of our minds, the pictures of home, family, a circle of friends, food, laughter, and gifts, it didn't begin that way. It started just off Main Street, in back of a cheap hotel, far from home and friends, with the sounds of bargaining and coarse conversation intermingled with the shuffling and settling of animals. Raise a sign over the manger: "God Is Love: Jesus Saves."

Salvation is one of the crucial words of the Christian faith. And when we read the Christmas story, the word confronts us at every turn.

When the angel hosts appeared to the shepherds outside Bethlehem, they announced, "To you is born this day in the city of David a Savior, who is Christ the Lord" (Luke 2:11). This was the "good news of a great joy": One had come who would save humanity.

And when an angel came to Joseph to explain the mystery of Mary's being with child, here was the statement that was used to describe the child Mary was to bear: "He will save his people from their sins" (Matthew 1:21b). For this he was born; for this he came into the world, that he might save.

Indeed, here is the very meaning of his name. A heavenly messenger declared that his name should be Jesus. It was a fairly common name in Israel, a name beloved among the Jews of that day. It meant "The Lord is salvation."

Years later, when Jesus tried to defend his conduct to the religious leaders who were critical of him for associating with sinners, he did so by giving a one-sentence summary of his mission: "'The Son of man came to seek and to save the lost'" (Luke 19:10).

The fact is, we cannot understand the Christmas season, the angel song, the mood of the New Testament, or the name of Jesus Christ without taking the word *salvation* to heart.

Save is a dramatic word. Think of the pictures it brings to mind: someone jumping into a body of water to rescue a drowning person, or perhaps someone running into a burning building to carry another to safety. Sometimes we use it in an economic sense, as when a person says, "So-and-so saved me from bankruptcy."

More than a hundred years ago, William Sleeper wrote a poem to describe his salvation.

> Out of my bondage, sorrow and night,
> Jesus, I come, Jesus, I come;
> Into Thy freedom, gladness, and light,
> Jesus, I come to Thee;
> Out of my sickness, into Thy health,
> Out of my want and into Thy wealth,
> Out of my sin and into Thyself,
> Jesus, I come to Thee.[1]

But I knew a man who chose to change the focus of the words. He was a bright, young scholar from a fine family and became a missionary much as another boy might become a businessman, primarily because it was his father's life. Still, he was without a personal religious faith, even though he was involved in religious work. His life began to collapse around him. He became depressed and at last suffered a severe nervous breakdown.

There in his lostness, Christ became a reality to him. He became a new man, one of the most beautiful I've ever known. Speaking from his experience, he insisted that he must speak the poem this way:

> Into my bondage, sorrow, and night,
> Jesus has come, Jesus has come;

Bringing His freedom, gladness, and light,
Jesus has come to me.

That is what God did at Christmas. To save someone, you must move into their need. If a lifeguard is to rescue a child from drowning, he must himself plunge into the water. The fireman puts his own life in peril as he hurtles into the burning building. The doctor and nurse walk into the epidemic, putting their own lives in danger. You don't save someone while standing at a safe, remote distance.

"Jesus Saves," the sign said. But he didn't do so by remaining in heavenly security. "And the Word became flesh and dwelt among us" (John 1:14a). He came to where we human creatures live: to the manger at a poor hotel in a sleepy town called Bethlehem, where people worried about the price of mutton and mothers baked bread and made a daily trip to the well. He comes to where the need is: a forsaken street, punctuated by pawn shops and cheap cafes; a lonely home where a woman worries about her son; an executive suite where a man wrestles with a hard decision; a high school bathroom where someone is trying to peddle drugs. He comes to both our inner cities and our suburbs. He comes to where we are.

For in order to save someone, you must move into their peril, their pain, their need. And therein is the Christmas story. God moved into our world, our lost human world, to save us. "Call his name Jesus, for he will save his people from their sins" (Matthew 1:21).

December 26

The Day After Christmas

*P*erhaps the most important thing about Christmas Day is the day after Christmas.

Unfortunately, however, the day after Christmas rarely gets much attention. The days before Christmas—and especially the night before Christmas—have attracted our fancy, and Christmas Day itself is sure to be exciting. But the day after Christmas is for most people an anticlimax, a letdown, perhaps even a disappointment.

Understand that I am not speaking simply of December 26th, the twenty-four hours immediately following Christmas Day. Nor am I referring to the tragic perversion of Christmas, which for some people makes the day after Christmas a day of coping with a hangover. I'm not even speaking of that time shortly after Christmas when our mailboxes bulge with bills, just as they bulged some days before with greeting cards.

No, I am speaking of something much bigger. At Christmas, something special ought to happen to us: a new sense of the nearness of God, a new love for our fellow human creatures, a new and larger giving of ourselves to God. Christmas ought, in some measure, to mean one or several of these things—an enlarging and a transforming of life. But what about the day after Christmas? What about the routine to which we return after the special moment is past?

Have you ever wondered what happened on the day after the first Christmas? All our Christmas pageants and most of our Christmas imaginings and musings center on the manger scene: shepherds and wise men kneeling before the newborn Babe. We can feel the magic of that moment: we sense its reverence, its eternal mystery. We envision the rugged shepherds, their heads bowed in reverence; we can see the wise men placing their gifts before the manger, just as we have seen it enacted scores of times in Christmas pageants. And just then, always, the curtain drops and a benediction is pronounced.

But the New Testament doesn't drop the curtain so soon. It gives us no detail, but it reminds us that there had to be a day after Christmas. "And the shepherds returned, glorifying and praising God for all they had heard and seen" (Luke 2:20). "And being warned in a dream not to return to Herod, [the wise men] departed to their own country by another way" (Matthew 2:12).

Some things would be the same. The shepherds would return to their work, and the wise men would return to their own country. But some things would be different. I think the difference can be summed up this way: for the shepherds and the wise men, Christmas meant a death and a new life. And so does every real Christmas.

The New Testament tells us that Herod had asked the wise men to return to him when they had found the newborn King. But after they had seen the Christ Child, we read that they went into their own country "another way." My Lord, another way indeed! We always go home another way after we have really experienced Christmas. Have you considered how greatly the wise men were changing their pattern of life in their going home by a different route? These men had been conditioned through all of their lives to be obedient to a king. They knew that their livelihood and, indeed, their very lives depended on such obedience. But now a new factor had come into their living, and they were proceeding in a fashion that was contradictory to all they had ever known.

Hear me: if you meet God, at Christmas or at any other season, you cannot come away from the event without a death. You will find, inevitably, that he has laid a hand on some aspect of your conduct, your thinking, your decision-making, and your style of life. Your attitude toward your money or your job or your treatment of people is likely to die, and a new way of living rises in its place.

But if Christmas means a death, it also means a new life. The shepherds returned to family and fields, "glorifying and praising God for all they had heard and seen." A new quality had come into their lives. They were men for whom each day was largely the same as the last. But now there was a glory, a brilliance, in their lives. So, too, it was with the wise men. The reason they could dare to reject a king's command was because they had a new King. The reason they could forfeit the advantages that King Herod's friendship might mean was because they had found a new advantage, an eternal one. The reason they could hazard the prospect of death was because they had found life. Something in them had died, but only because a marvelous new life had pushed into its place.

So now, for you and me, it is the day after Christmas. If your Christmas was only gifts and cards and celebrations and music, I won't disparage it, for heaven knows we need such a light in our skies. But it isn't enough. Christmas ought to mean a death: the death of some attitudes and conduct that are less than God would have them be. And it ought to mean a birth: a new birth to new life in Jesus Christ.

I hope you had a beautiful day yesterday. I pray that this season has brought much gladness, much friendship, much love and laughter into your life. But where do you go from here? Will you be a better human being because of Christmas? Will something from this season make you different, wonderfully different, in the days to come?

God grant that it may be so for you.

Christmas Word: Sanctification

Sanctification is the word after Christmas. The Shorter Catechism defines sanctification as "the work of God's free grace, whereby we are ...enabled more and more to die unto sin, and live unto righteousness."[1] What a right word for this spot on the calendar. It isn't enough to have a warm heart, wonderful and blessed as that may be. We need to go on to perfection. We need to be sanctified. Just as one year is dying out, may we also "die unto sin"; and as a new year is born, may we begin with new gladness to "live unto righteousness." Sanctification comes from the Latin word *sanctus*, which means "holy." Sanctification is a first cousin to the word *sanctuary*. A sanctuary is a holy place, and sanctification is the establishing of a holy life. A sanctified person is someone who has been set apart by God, someone who is special because of holiness. In other words, a sanctified person is a saint.

Now you might be thinking, "Obviously this has nothing to do with me, because I'm no saint," but I must argue the point with you. If you are a sincere Christian, trying with some degree of earnestness to follow Christ, you are what the New Testament calls a saint. The Roman Catholic Church has given a special quality to the name, by selecting some people through an intricate process who it then identifies as saints. But the New Testament is more democratic: saints are not a spiritual aristocracy, as G. Campbell Morgan once put it, they are all who are Christians.

That may be something of a disappointment. Groucho Marx once said that he would never join a club that would invite a fellow like him to be a member. Such may be your reaction when you discover you're a saint: if folks like you qualify, perhaps sainthood isn't such a big deal.

But believe me, it is. Two factors are involved. On the one hand, sanctification is something God has done. It is a fact accomplished, like being born, and it has little to do with one's own achievements. Thus the apostle Paul began his letter to the church at Corinth by addressing them as "saints," yet he spent most of the letter dealing with their shortcomings. In calling them "saints" he was referring to what God had done in their lives. He was speaking of their holy potential. When he exhorted them to better living, he was stirring them to live up to their name.

Perhaps I can describe it this way. When a child is born in our country, we say that he or she is an American citizen even though the child doesn't vote, doesn't pay taxes, and doesn't serve his country. Nevertheless, we call the child a citizen. We hope that someday he or she will "deserve" the name, but meanwhile the title is true. Thus, when we become Christians we are "sanctified," set apart for a holy purpose, and even if we fall short of that purpose, the word still applies.

Nevertheless, sanctification is something in which we ought to cooperate. Having been identified as citizens of the heavenly kingdom, we want to live up to our citizenship. A good work was begun in us when we were converted, but it was only a beginning. The prayer for sanctification is a prayer that God will finish this work, that he will lead us on to the fullness of life, which was implicit in our salvation.

The process is partly in our hands and partly in God's. On the night before his crucifixion, Jesus told his followers that their lives must be pruned and cut away, just as the branches of a fruit tree are pruned. The purpose is that our lives should be more fruitful; and although pruning seems a painful process, it is worth it.

Indeed, as we seek sanctification, we can encourage ourselves with the knowledge that God is on our side. When we go after saintliness, we pursue something for which we were created. God meant a good and high life for us. The world and the tide of the times may oppose and frustrate our seeking, but God and the quality he has planted within us both pull us toward our goal.

Our world needs many things, but nothing more than saints. In Matthew 5:13 Jesus called such "the salt of the earth"—that is, that which preserves life and gives it quality and flavor. We need such life preservers and enrichers. Without them the quality of life will deteriorate until it is not worth saving.

Whatever other goal we may have for the new year, let us set this primary one: we will go on to perfection. We were made for such an achievement, and God has willed that we should have it. *Sanctification* is the word that completes Christmas and fulfills its potential. Jesus came, not simply to bless us with the joy and beauty of one memorable day, but to make it possible for us to become saints.

December 28

Ain't Gonna Study
War No More

Christmas is the season of song. Yet for all of the wide variety of songs we sing and hear at this time of year, this old spiritual probably doesn't come to mind. "Ain't Gonna Study War No More" doesn't seem to us like Christmas music. But when the song declares, "Gonna lay down my sword and shield, down by the riverside. Ain't gonna study war no more," I tell you that is Christmas music.

If I asked a hundred passing people the meaning of Christmas, a substantial number would say, "Peace on earth, goodwill toward men." With such an answer, they may miss the theological heart of Christmas, but they will reflect the element in the Christmas story that appeals to them most. We see that phrase, "Peace on earth," on scores of Christmas cards each year, as well as "Prince of Peace" on many others. This is the season when the cry for peace becomes most insistent, and most hopeful. At Christmastime, we believe that peace might really be possible.

The old spiritual not only fits the Christmas mood of peace, it does so with profound good sense. The language of the song goes surely to the heart of the matter. Our trouble begins, you see, with the fact that we study war. War has commanded our attention.

Think, for example, of the historical dates that you remember. Are they not the dates of war: 1066 (the Battle of Hastings, with William the Conqueror), 1776 (the Revolutionary War), 1812 (the War of 1812), 1861–65 (the Civil War), 1914–18 (World War I), December 7, 1941 (Pearl Harbor, which drew the United States into World War II)? These are the sorts of dates from history that are embedded in our minds. We've studied war. We've hung the story of human history on the crucifying dates of war.

Or think of the names that stand out in world history: Alexander the Great, Julius Caesar, Napoleon Bonaparte, and Adolf Hitler. You may not like or admire them, but you'll include their names in your catalog of memory.

So the spiritual is wonderfully wise when it vows, "I ain't gonna study war no more." I don't know where the unknown author got his or her insight, but he or she might surely have been thinking of the words found in two Old Testament prophets, Isaiah and Micah: "And they shall beat their swords into plowshares, and their spears into pruning hooks; nation shall not lift up sword against nation, neither shall they learn war any more" (Isaiah 2:4b; Micah 4:3b).

Some devoutly religious people have not been sure they should work for peace, because Jesus said that in the last days our world will have "wars and rumors of wars" (Matthew 24:6; Mark 13:7). They have wondered if they might be opposing God's action in history by efforts for peace. But the answer is in Jesus's own words in Matthew 5:9, "'Blessed are the peacemakers.'" Whatever the prophecy of war, our assignment is to work for peace. We need not speculate on how God's ultimate plans will fit together when his command for us is so certain. He has called us to be peacemakers.

Peacemaking is not an easy business, but the difficulty does not excuse us from trying. Indeed, it only demands that we try still harder. When the Quakers came to Delaware in 1682, it was under the banner, "Now let us try what love will do." We are obligated, for our own sakes and out of our loyalty to the Prince of Peace, to see what we can do by studying peace, rather than war.

We can begin in the home. It is a lesson as simple as the toys with which children play, the books they read, and the heroes who capture their affection. It is a matter of the television shows our children watch, the movies we let them see. And surely it is also the language they hear. How can we learn peace if so much of our daily communication is in the language of hostility?

We can do a better job in the schools. We should give our children more information about the great heroes of peace. We don't have to discredit past heroes in order to do so. Some of America's greatest military leaders took their role unwillingly. General Robert E. Lee wrote his wife, "What a cruel thing is war: to separate and destroy families and friends and mar the purest joys and happiness God has granted us in this world."[1] General Douglas MacArthur, considered by many to have been the greatest military genius of our history, worked to put a nonmilitary provision in the constitution of the new Japan. General Dwight Eisenhower warned us of the evil of the military-industrial complex. Schoolchildren should know that many military leaders have become the most passionate advocates of peace because they knew so well the insanity of war.

We should study our own motives and the spirit in which we work as well. It is so easy to lose sight of a cause even as we work for it. I have seen a lot of hateful conduct and heard a good deal of violent language in the support of peace. It's almost as if people have to have somebody to hate, even while they speak of peace.

So peace is not easy to come by. Not only do we have to convince our opponents, we have to convince our own souls. War and destruction have centuries of history on their side, not only in fact, but also in our thoughts. At this season, therefore, we need to become reacquainted with the Prince of Peace. We need to see him not only as someone the world should know, or that our enemies should know, but that we ought to know.

So let us sing it, friend: "I ain't gonna study war no more." Instead, we will seek to learn from the Prince of Peace.

December 29

Of Parlors and Stables

When the innkeeper turned away Joseph and Mary and the Savior of the world, they were not completely shut out. Room was made for them. The parlor and the guest rooms were filled, but there was room in the stable. And this, surely, is where the innkeeper is like you and me.

When I was still in my teens, an attorney spelled out the issue for me. He was a man's man, as he put it, so when anyone visited his home, he made it a point to show them his den with its collection of guns, trophies, and mounted animals. But then he became a deeply convinced Christian, and for the first time he realized the issue of life's parlor and stable. His own masculinity was on prominent display in the parlor, and his Christian faith had been pushed out into the stable, back where no one would find it without looking.

And how about you and me? What occupies the parlor in our lives? When someone comes to know you, what do they find in your parlor, as evidenced by your conversation, your enthusiasm, or the way you spend your money? And where is Jesus? Is he in the living room, at the heart and glory of your life; or is he out in the stable, crowded out by other things that, in truth, matter more to you?

I'm sure you understand that I'm not urging you to make a show of your religion. That would be hypocrisy. I'm asking where Jesus really ranks in your life—and that's Christianity. I'm talking about priorities. Many things are good, but they are not to be ranked first. Many things belong in our lives, but we shouldn't belong to them.

Our priorities show themselves in so many ways, some subtle and some obvious. When we complain that we haven't time to read the Bible or a devotional book, but we spend hours a week with the news, we show what we put in the parlor and what we put in the stable. Our budget and our checkbooks are a dramatic indication. And it's not simply a matter of how much we invest in the several enterprises of our lives, but also the mood in which we do it. As you look at your checkbook, would you say that Christ is in the parlor of your life, or is he subsisting out in the stable? And our use of time: is your life filled up with so many things that Christ is usually housed in the stable, in what's left?

Of course you and I do give him some room. We acknowledge him at least somewhat. But much of the time, in the daily business of living, we house him in the stable. We give him what's left. The parlor we reserve for another.

Understand me: I'm not saying that Christ should take the place of your work, your school studies, your social life, or your community involvement. Far, far from it. I'm saying that he should become Lord of life—Lord of your work, your schooling, your social activities, and your community interests. In each of those settings, he is the One we serve. In each of those areas of responsibility, he is the One we aim to please.

Jesus Christ does not belong in the stable of our lives. Above all, he should be in the parlor; for he is the only One who really fits there.

You and I have one edge on the innkeeper. As far as we know he got only one opportunity to provide lodging for Jesus the Christ. You and I have a grand opportunity this day, this season in which we celebrate his birth. And we have a chance to underline our choice every day, in the business of living. As a matter of fact, the opportunity is thrust upon us. We have to decide. Again and again, we decide whether the Lord of life shall reside in our stable, or whether we want him in our parlor.

On Losing the Star

$\mathcal{C}$hristmas ought to remind us that we're always in danger of losing the star. You remember, of course, how crucial the star was in the story of the first Christmas. Wise men from the East, who were students of the stars and their movements, somehow became impressed that a spectacular heavenly formation was heralding the birth of a king of the Jews, and they set out to visit him.

When you stop to think of it, it's a strange story. You see, they weren't simply following a star, they were following it on the basis of a very specific revelation: that it would lead them to the newborn King of the Jews. But then why should they be concerned about a king for the Jews? They were not Jewish themselves, yet they were concerned enough to make a long, perilous journey to see him. Moreover, the Jews were a captive people, an exceedingly modest and somewhat unpopular minority in the vast Roman Empire. They hadn't really had a government of their own for generations, and they hadn't been a power to be reckoned with for eight or nine hundred years, since the time of David and Solomon. Why go to see a possible King of the Jews? What would he matter if they found him?

But they set out to find him, and eventually did so; and the wise men have ever since been a part of poem, story, tradition, legend, and song. Probably half of the men in any congregation have at some time in their lives dressed in a bathrobe and sandals to be a wise man in a church or school pageant.

But, in that magnificent story, one part is often missed; almost always, in fact. Apparently the wise men lost the star somewhere in the midst of their journey. They got as far as Jerusalem, and they then began making inquiry throughout the city. At last the chief priests and scribes there told them that the Messiah-King was, according to prophecy, to be born in Bethlehem of Judea. So they set out on their journey again; and now, "the star which they had seen in the East went before them, till it came to rest over the place where the child was. When they saw the star, they rejoiced exceedingly with great joy" (Matthew 2:9b-10).

Obviously, you see, something happened. Either they lost faith in the star, and thus sought information—or confirmation—in Jerusalem among scholars and theologians, or else they simply lost sight of the star and didn't know where to go. At any rate, eventually the star reappeared . . . or their faith in it returned and they came to their destination.

We're always in danger of losing the star. So often in life we catch a great dream, a special vision, and we set out to find it or to bring it to fulfillment. And then, somewhere, we lose it.

I'm sure that's one of the special problems of this season itself. Most of us can remember the special excitement of childhood

Christmas—a pure, unadulterated excitement. Some of us resolved, in those days, that we would make Christmas better for everybody when we were adults and able to accomplish great things. Have we remembered those dreams?

I can remember Depression Christmases. There was a magic to Christmas, even with next to nothing. Isn't it surprising—and upsetting—that we don't appreciate Christmas now, with abundance, as much as we appreciated it then, with little? Have we lost the star?

And this happens, you know, with our personal relationships. I think of it when I see young people preparing to marry, full of stars in their eyes . . . I wonder if they will someday lose the stars and take their spouse for granted?

At this point in our lives, we ought to ask ourselves about the idealism of our youth. We had stars in our eyes then; we followed a star, for sure! Have you lost it? Have you settled into comfortable affluence, embarrassed that once you thought you'd fight for great causes?

What about your faith? You might remember a moment of vision in youth . . . an hour when you realized your dedication to God. It was at a church service, or a scout camp, or a quiet night. Have you lost the star? Or do you still have that same bright faith?

I Believe in Tomorrow

I believe in tomorrow.

In a sense, everybody believes in tomorrow—that's why we go on living. And yet a great many people only accept tomorrow because they see no alternative. They don't want to die, but they have no vital impulse to live.

Indeed, many people dread their tomorrows. Vast numbers of people look forward to sleeping at night with the feeling that it will mean relief from the physical and psychological pain of the waking hours. Many people awaken in the morning sick at heart at what the day holds for them: they are afraid of their jobs, or they dread meeting the people with whom they have to work, or they don't know how to cope with their families. Falling asleep at night is for them like a pleasant retreat into the womb of life, and awakening in the morning is a violent reminder that there is a life to be faced.

No, some people don't believe in tomorrow. And when the "tomorrow" of which we speak is not simply the next twenty-four-hour period, but a new year, their apprehension is intensified. This is painfully demonstrated by the fact that the year's end always brings a sudden increase in suicides. Apparently some people who have struggled through a year simply feel overwhelmed when they consider the prospect of another year of the same struggle—so they give up.

But I'm glad for tomorrow, because tomorrow means a new start. Most of us are dissatisfied with some aspect of a day as it comes to its close, and we like to think that we can improve on that day tomorrow. Sometimes it is simply work undone, and we close the day saying, "Well, tomorrow's another day"—which means that perhaps we will "make the grade" tomorrow.

Surely one of God's great, recurring blessings is contained in the fact that life is broken into predictable segments by the movement of the planets. If life were only an endless sheet, with no page to turn and no point for a new departure, it would surely be too much to manage. Instead, life comes to us in little pieces—we often use the imagery of a book and call the pieces "leaves." When the piece called "today" is smeared by our errors, we say hopefully, "Tomorrow I'll turn over a new leaf."

The "new leaf" is much easier to bring to pass precisely because the calendar cooperates with us. We are so much more able to make a new start when something about the structuring of time puts some kind of wall around the past.

I think it is important—very important—to believe in tomorrow. Because what tomorrow is, actually, is not half as important as what I think of it. Tomorrow is not quite a neutral quality, but certainly it is ours for the shaping. Tomorrow may, in fact, be almost black in prospect; but if I come to it with light and hope, I can at the least make it gray and perhaps even bright. On the other hand, tomorrow may, in fact, be full of promise; but if I come to it with despair, I can soon make it over in my own image.

So I choose to believe in tomorrow. I think it is important to do so, as a strategy for dealing with life. But I don't believe in tomorrow simply as a strategy. I believe in it because I believe in God.

I believe that tomorrow is a creature of God's making. It may already seem misshapen as it comes to my hand, because of the crucible of life in which I find it; but tomorrow is of itself a part of God's good creation. It comes from his hand a beautiful thing, rich in opportunity. I believe that tomorrow is, by its origin in God, geared entirely for good. I have reason to hope for tomorrow because of the God from whom it comes.

And I believe in tomorrow because I believe in God's ability to redeem and transform human life. If not, I would know that tomorrow would be doomed to be very much like today; somewhat better, perhaps, because being a day older I am also a day wiser, but somewhat worse, perhaps, because being a day older I am also a day weaker.

On January, 1, 1797, Horatio Nelson wrote his father from his ship in the Mediterranean: "My dear Father, on this day I am certain you will send me a letter." Dr. Henry Sloane Coffin said, upon reading young Nelson's letter, "Sons and daughters of a far more devoted and faithful Father can surely look up, as we stand at the outset of another stretch of life's untried way, and tell Him: 'On this day I am certain Thou hast a word for me.'"[1] I think his word might be: Enter your tomorrow with a redeemed life; enter it with faith and thanksgiving. It will be better than yesterday and today.

And as for you—I believe in your tomorrow. Without knowing the condition of your health or the state of your bank balance; without knowing the frustration you have felt in your work or the disappointment you have met in your human relationships; without knowing your sins, your shame, your humiliation, your sense of failure—I believe in your tomorrow. For I believe in God and in his ability to redeem life. I am satisfied that he can make the rough places plain and bring the darkness to light. For your tomorrow comes from the hand of God.

Notes

December 3

1. A. C. Bouquet, *Everyday Life in New Testament Times* (New York: Scribner, 1954), 106.

2. Amos Russel Wells and Frances Brentano, eds., "The Inn That Missed Its Chance," in *The Light of Christmas* (New York: Dutton, 1964).

December 5

1. Editorial, "The Merchant's Side," *Scott County Times* (Forest, MS), Nov. 30, 1966.

December 9

1. Charles Wesley, "Come, Thou Long-Expected Jesus," *The United Methodist Hymnal* (Nashville: The United Methodist Publishing House, 1989), 196.

2. Isaac Watts, "Joy to the World," *The United Methodist Hymnal* (Nashville: The United Methodist Publishing House, 1989), 246.

December 10

1. Alexander Maclaren, "Expositions of Holy Scripture Ephesians, Peter, John," Bible Hub (website), http://biblehub.com/library/maclaren/expositions _of_holy_scripture_ephesians_peter/salvation_grace_faith.htm.

December 12

1. William Barclay, *Barclay on the Lectionary: Mark, Year B* (Edinburgh: Saint Andrew Press, 2014), 92.

December 13

1. George Buttrick, ed., *The Interpreter's Bible: A Commentary in Twelve Volumes*, vol. 7, *New Testament Articles, Matthew, Mark* (New York and Nashville: Abingdon-Cokesbury Press, 1951), 259.

December 14

1. W. E. Sangster, *Sangster's Special-Day Sermons* (Grand Rapids, MI: Baker, 1960), 17.

December 20

1. Madeleine L'Engle, *The Irrational Season* (New York: Seabury, 1977), 18.

December 21

1. Paul Tillich and Whit Burnett, eds., *Spirit of Man* (New York: Hawthorn, 1958), 261.

2. Tillich and Burnett, *Spirit of Man*, 258.

December 22

1. John H. Hopkins Jr., "We Three Kings," *The United Methodist Hymnal* (Nashville: The United Methodist Publishing House, 1989), 254.

December 25

1. William T. Sleeper, "Jesus, I Come," *Favorite Hymns of Praise* (Chicago: Tabernacle, 1972), 295.

December 27

1. Westminster Assembly, Douglas F. Kelly, Philip B. Rollinson, and Frederick T. Marsh, *The Westminster Shorter Catechism in Modern English* (Phillipsburg, NJ: Presbyterian and Reformed Pub. Co., 1986), Question 35.

December 28

1. Quoted in Charles Wallis, ed., *Our American Heritage* (New York: Harper and Row, 1970), 119.

December 31

1. Henry Sloane Coffin, *Joy in Believing* (New York: Scribner and Sons, 1956), 3.

BOOKS YOU MAY ALSO ENJOY

Christmas from the Back Side: A Different Look at the Story of Jesus' Birth
ISBN: 9780687027064

Look at the biblical story of Christmas through the "back side"—a unique starting point, a creative retelling, a new "lens," or the eyes of a minor character. The late J. Ellsworth Kalas's creative approach both clarifies basic teachings and introduces new possibilities of meaning to the Christmas story.

Easter from the Back Side also available.
ISBN: 9780687490790

When Did God Become a Christian?: Knowing God Through the Old and New Testaments
Book ISBN: 9781501830969
Leader Guide ISBN: 9781501830983

Join David Kalas as he identifies common experiences, troublesome passages, and natural reactions that we encounter while reconciling the God of both the Old and New Testaments. Explores the unity of Scripture, biblical history, and the two primary attributes of God—love and holiness—to help clarify the integrity of the nature of God.

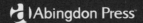